Beginning W

How to Make Books
with Children Series

Beginning Writers provides activities on 22 topics to stimulate and develop oral language and motivate the creation of picture or word stories. The structure of the lessons and the reproducible pages will enable you to meet the varied writing needs in your classroom from nonwriters to confident beginning writers.

Each of the 22 topics contains:

Resource Pages

- Literature recommendations
- Prewriting activities
- Suggestions for individual books
- Suggestions for group books

Reproducible Pages

- Book cover
- Blank form—Use for drawing a picture story and for a back cover
- Cloze form—Use to complete sentences
- Lined writing form
- Clip art—Use to enhance group book projects

Congratulations on your purchase of some of the finest teaching materials in the world.

For information about other Evan-Moor products, call 1-800-777-4362 or FAX 1-800-777-4332

Visit our website http://www.evan-moor.com. Check the Product Updates link for supplements, additions, and corrections for this book.

Author: Jo Ellen Moore
Editor: Marilyn Evans
Illustrator: Jo Larsen
Designer: Jo Larsen
Desktop: Jo Larsen
Cover design: Cheryl Puckett

EDUCATIONAL PUBLISHERS

EMC 776

Table of Contents

How to Use This Book

Prewriting Activities

Writing begins long before a pencil touches paper. The prewriting step is essential to the writing process. It is a time for asking questions, sharing ideas, enriching vocabulary, clarifying concepts, and gathering ideas. Each unit in *Beginning Writers* provides prewriting activities to prepare students for the writing experience.

- **Read to Your Class**

  A list of "read-aloud" selections is provided for each theme. Take advantage of this wonderful way to enrich language and develop new concepts.

- **Get Ready to Write**

  The teacher resource page for each theme suggests how to use real-life items to increase vocabulary and develop concepts. An important part of this step is brainstorming. Make a list of the words or ideas students share. This activity reinforces the relationship between the spoken and printed word.

Providing for All Writers

One of the advantages of this resource book is that the same theme can be used simultaneously with students of varying writing levels. Each student can successfully create a book whether it be a picture story, a completed-sentences story, or an independently written story.

- **Picture Stories**

  Blank forms are provided for picture stories. Each child thinks about what his or her story will be and then draws an appropriate picture on the blank forms. The cover is then stapled to the finished pages. Some students will add invented spelling to their drawings. Encourage these attempts at writing. (These blank forms are great for interactive writing activities.)

- **Complete the Sentences (Cloze Forms)**

  These forms provide a framework for a story. Reproduce a copy of a cover, a blank form, and the cloze form for each student. List words that might go in each blank. Students then complete the sentences in their own way and draw a picture on the blank form. Staple on the cover to complete the books.

- **Write a Story**

  Several story starters are provided for each theme. Assign a topic or allow students to choose. Reproduce a supply of the lined form. Students can write their stories using as many forms as they need.

Group Books

Two ideas for group books are provided for each theme. These books use the forms as the individual books. A page of clip art illustrations is provided for each theme. Suggestions are given for how to use the clip art in making a group book.

Sharing Student-Authored Books

Creating a book is an exciting experience for young writers. Provide opportunities for students to share their stories with others. Have them read their own stories to the class, send both individual and group books home to share with parents, and put student-authored books in the class library.

Putting Books Together

Each student will need a copy of the front cover and a blank form for the back cover. Some students may need help cutting out the forms. Group books will get a lot of use. Photocopy the covers on heavy paper or glue colored covers to card stock.

- **Staple**
  Staple the cover to the pages. Cover the staples with a strip of book tape.

- **Lace-up**
  Punch holes through the cover and pages.
  Lace the pages together with a shoelace, yarn, or string.

  1. Lace down through end holes.
  2. Lace up through middle holes.
  3. Tie on top.

- **Rings**
  Punch holes through the cover and pages. Put together with metal rings. (This is a good technique for thick books with cardboard covers.)

Other Uses for Reproducible Pages

Creating Class Books

Although book suggestions are given for each theme, the forms can be used to make your own books.

- Alphabet Books
- Category Books
- Letter-Sound Books
- Counting Books
- Story Books
- Poetry Books

Handwriting Practice

Use the reproducible lined pages for handwriting practice. Students may practice single letters or whole sentences. They may copy short poems using their best handwriting.

Using Cover Illustrations

Cover pages can be used to:

- decorate bulletin boards
- create covers for student work portfolios
- create students' journals
- make awards or announcements

Prewriting Activities

Read

The Doorbell Rang by Patricia Hutchins;
  Turtleback, 1989.
If You Give a Mouse a Cookie by Laura
  Joffe Numeroff; Harper Trophy, 1997.
Cookie Count by Robert Sabuda; Little
  Simon, 1997.
A Cow, a Bee, a Cookie and Me by
  Meredith Hooper; Kingfisher Books, 1997.
Who Stole the Cookies? by Judith Moffatt;
  Grosset & Dunlap, 1996.
*The Gingerbread Man: An Old English
  Folktale* by John A. Rowe; North South
  Books, 1996.
*Gus and Grandpa and the Christmas
  Cookies* by Claudia Mills; Farrar, Straus
  & Giroux, 1997.

Get Ready to Write

1. Brainstorm and list all of the different kinds
   of cookies students can name.

2. Bring in a variety of types of cookies. Have
   students describe attributes of the cookies
   (shape, color, size, contents, taste, etc.).
   Extend the activity by graphing students'
   favorite cookies.

Writing Activities

Individual Books

- **Draw a Story**

  Reproduce the cover and several blank pages. Help students think of their own topics for stories or use one of the following ideas:

  My Favorite Cookies
  Draw a different cookie on each form.

  How to Make a Cookie
  Draw pictures to show the steps for making a cookie.

- **Complete the Sentences**

  Reproduce the cover, a blank form, and the cloze form. Students complete the sentences to create a story and then draw a picture on the blank form.

- **Write a Story**

  Reproduce the cover and several lined writing forms. Students write their own cookie stories. Possible story starters:

Why I Like Cookies	*Cookies in My Lunch Box*
A _____ Stole My Cookie	*How to Make a Cookie*
The Magic Cookie	*Cookie Crumbs under My Bed*

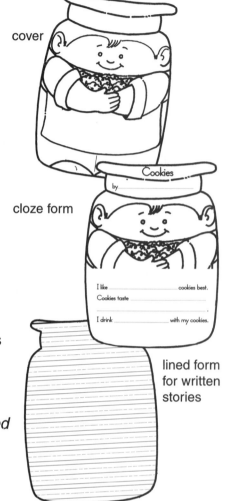

cover

cloze form

I like _____ cookies best.
Cookies taste _____
I drink _____ with my cookies.

lined form for written stories

Group Books

- **A Cookie Counting Book**

  Give each student a blank cookie jar form and one or more copies of the cookie clip art page. Assign each student a number. Students color, cut out the correct number of cookie shapes, and paste them to the blank form. Students then write a phrase or sentence on the bottom of the page to describe the cookies shown. Arrange the pages in numerical order and staple with a copy of the cover on top.

- **"Starts Like Cookie"**

  The cookie clip art may also be used for a book about objects that begin with the /k/ sound of the letter "c." Students will need a blank cookie jar form and several cookie shapes. Draw a picture of something starting with the sound /k/ on each cookie, glue the cookies to the blank cookie jar form, and write the name of each object by its picture. Compile student pages and attach a cover.

3 sugar cookies in the jar

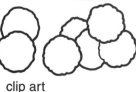

clip art

8

Note: Reproduce this book cover for each student.

9

Note: Reproduce this page to draw a picture story or to use as a back cover.

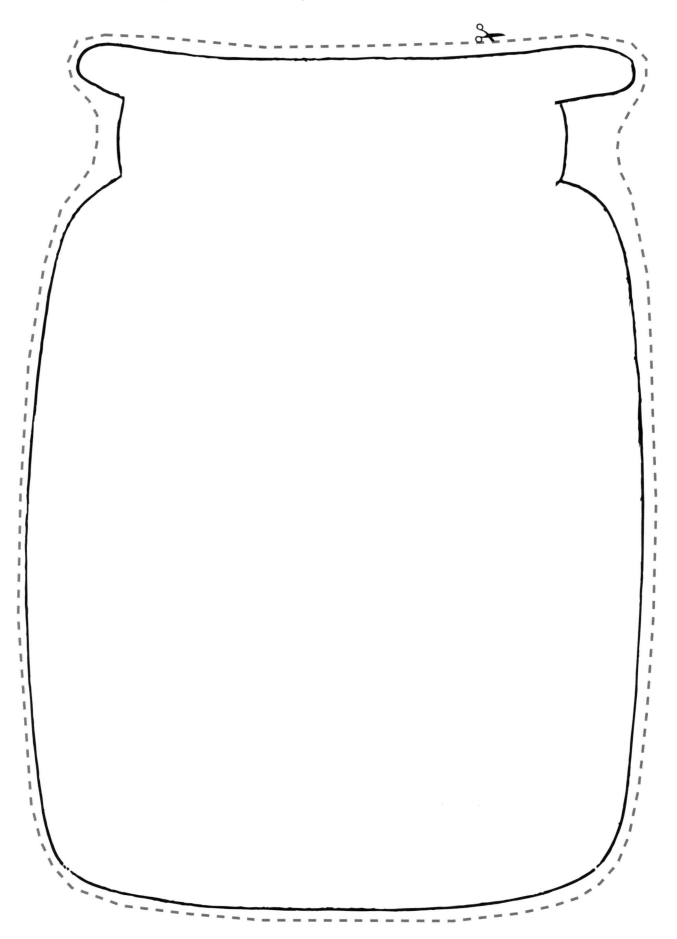

Beginning Writers • EMC 776

Cookies

by _____

I like _____ cookies best.

Cookies taste _____

_____ .

I drink _____ with my cookies.

Note: Reproduce this page for written stories.

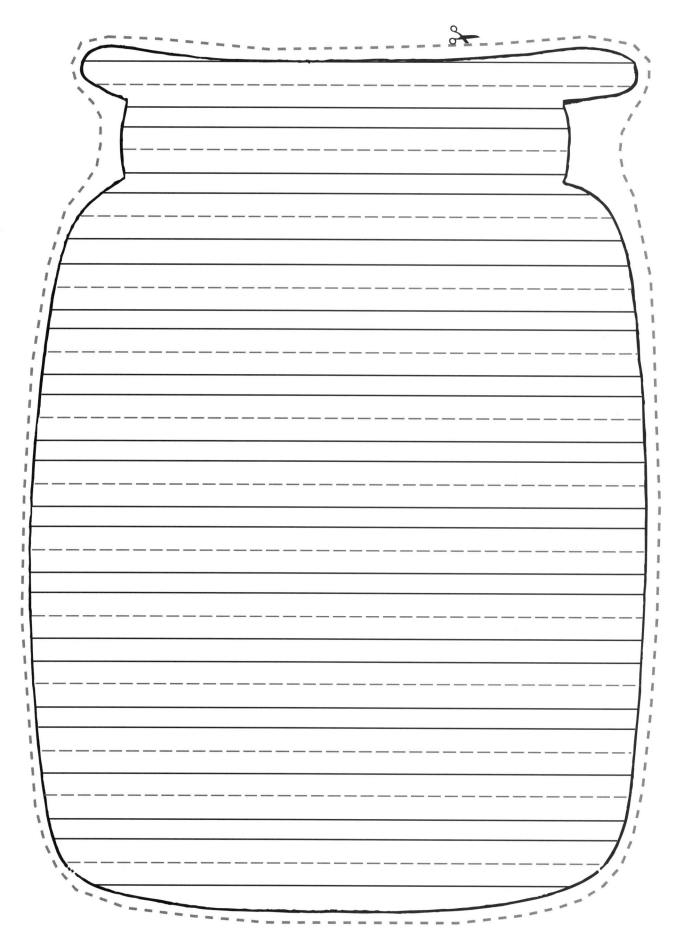

12

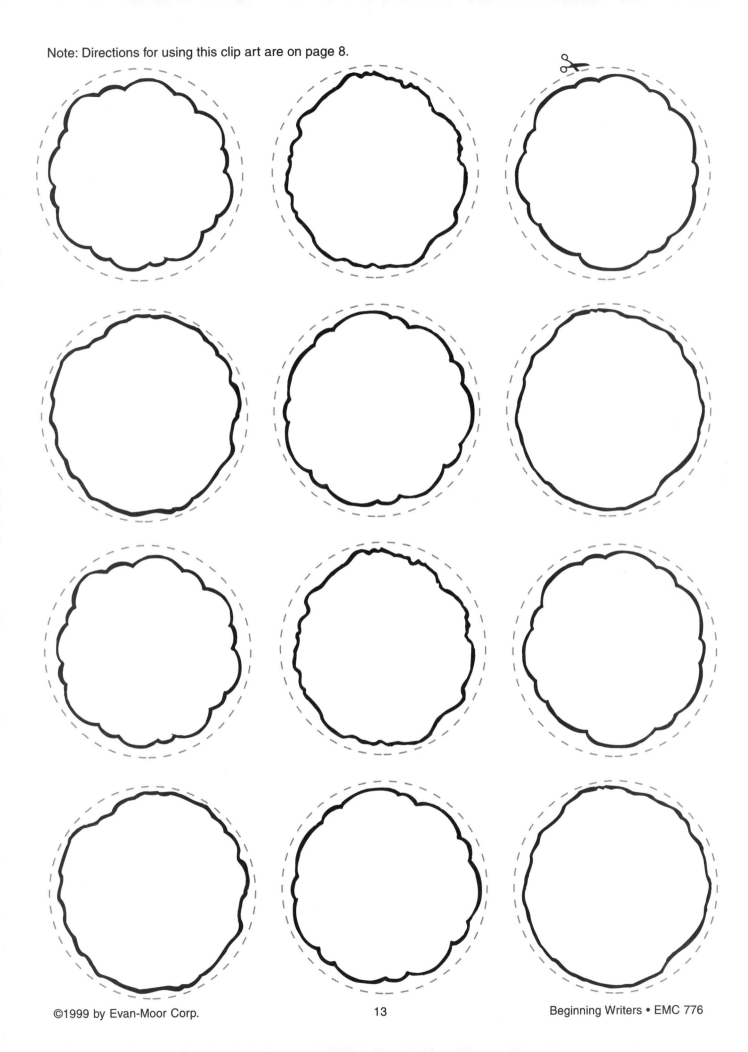

Prewriting Activities

Read

Alexander, Who Used to Be Rich Last Sunday by Judith Viorst; Turtleback, 1980.

A Dollar for Penny by Julie Glass; Random House, 1998.

Benny's Pennies by Pat Brisson; Yearling Books, 1995.

Charlotte's Piggy Bank by David McKee; Andersen Press Ltd., 1996.

A Chair for My Mother by Vera B. Williams; Greenwillow, 1984.

Get Ready to Write

1. Bring in a collection of real banks and coins for your students to explore. Ask how many of them have a bank and/or save money.

2. Brainstorm the things students would like, for which they would need to save money. (Set a time limit or let each student name one special thing they would like.) Talk about where they will get the money to save.

Writing Activities

Individual Books

- **Draw a Story**
  Reproduce the cover and several blank pages.
  Help students think of their own topics for
  stories or use one of the following ideas:

  If I Had a Dollar
  Students draw an item on each page that could
  be purchased with a dollar. Color the piggy bank
  cover, adding an interesting pattern or design.

  In My Piggy Bank
  Students draw one thing on each piggy bank
  page (these objects can be coins or something
  unusual). Color the piggy bank cover, adding an
  interesting pattern or design.

- **Complete the Sentences**
  Reproduce the cover, a blank form, and the cloze
  form. Students complete the sentences to create
  a story and then draw a picture on the blank form.

- **Write a Story**
  Reproduce the cover and several lined forms.
  Students write their own piggy bank stories.
  Possible story starters:

At the Toy Store	*Inside My Piggy Bank*
How Can I Get Some Money?	*My (kind of bank) Bank*
The Broken Piggy Bank	*The Sad Piggy Bank*

cover

cloze form

In My Piggy Bank
by _____

I have _____ cents.
I am saving money to get _____.

I can buy it at _____.

lined form for
written stories

Group Books

- **How Much Money Is in My Bank?**
  Give each student a copy of the blank pig form and the money
  clip art. Students are to cut out the coins and paste a money
  amount on the piggy bank form. Students then dictate or
  write, "I have _____ cents in my piggy bank." Compile
  student pages and attach a cover.

- **The Talking Piggy Bank**
  Give each student one or more lined forms. Discuss the kinds
  of things a piggy bank might say if it could talk. Then have
  students write their own talking piggy
  bank stories. Compile student pages
  and attach a cover.

I have 76¢ in my piggy bank.

clip art

Note: Reproduce this book cover for each student.

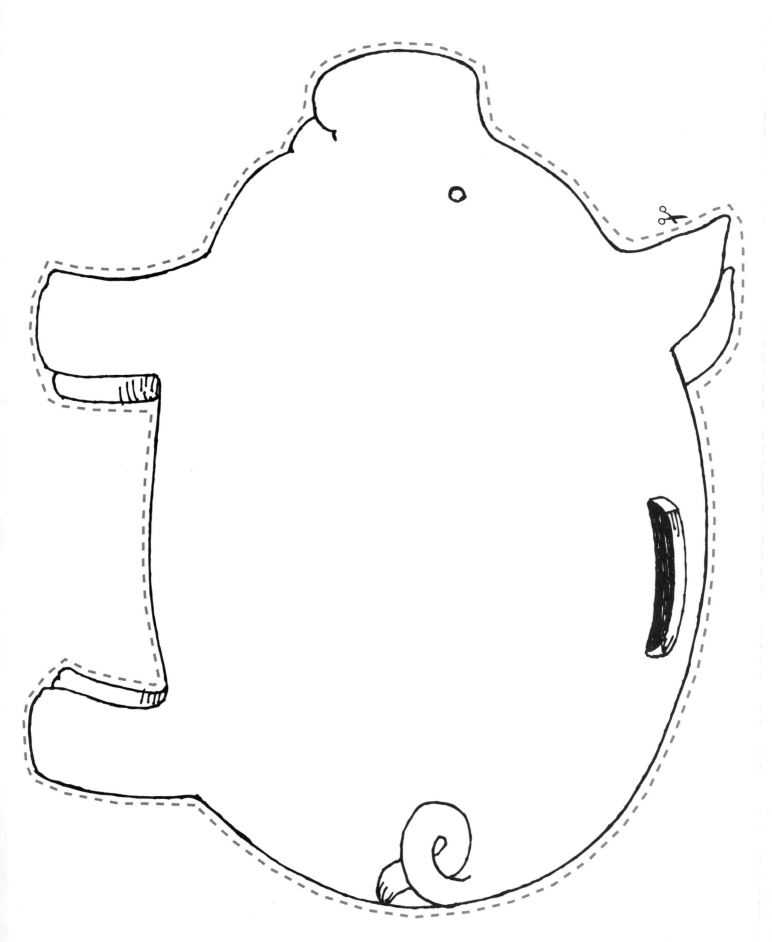

 Beginning Writers • EMC 776

Note: Reproduce this page to draw a picture story or to use as a back cover.

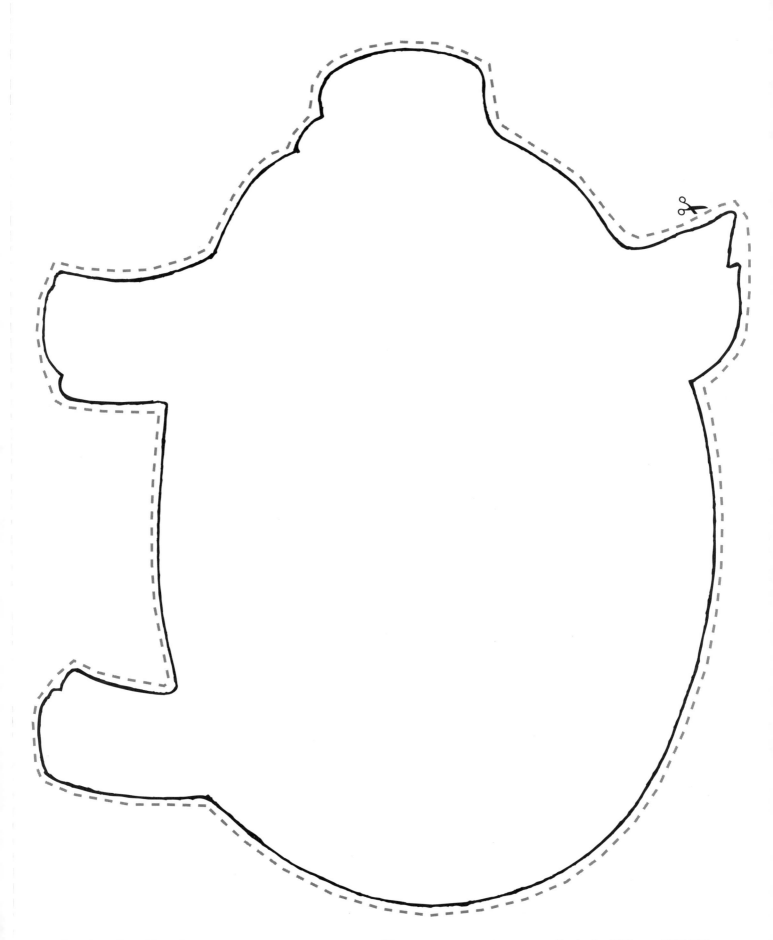

17

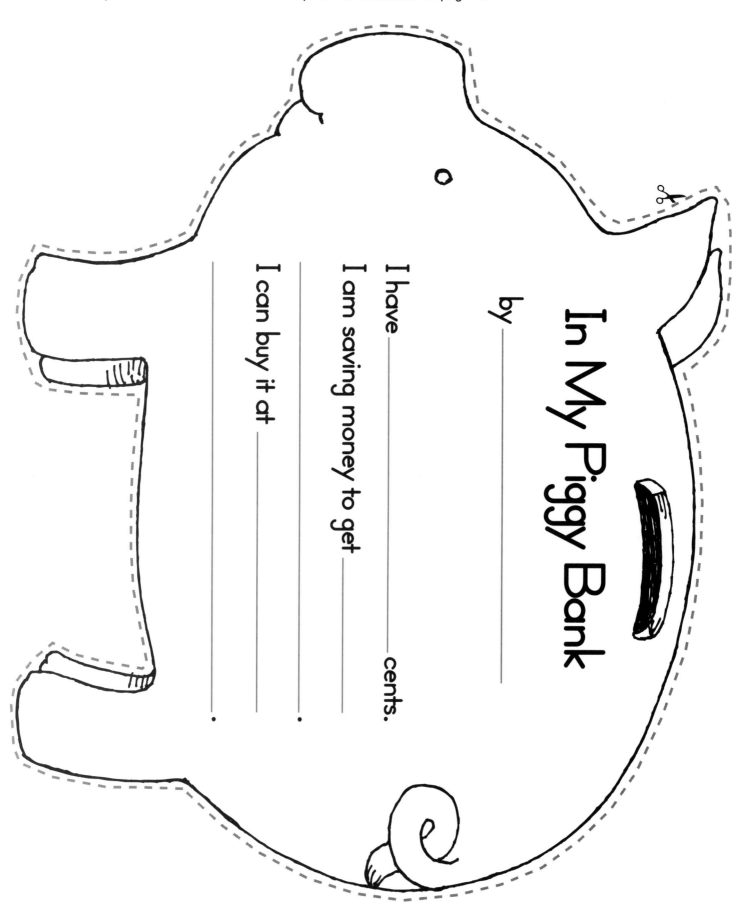

In My Piggy Bank

by _____

I have _____ cents.

I am saving money to get _____

I can buy it at _____ .

Note: Reproduce this page for written stories.

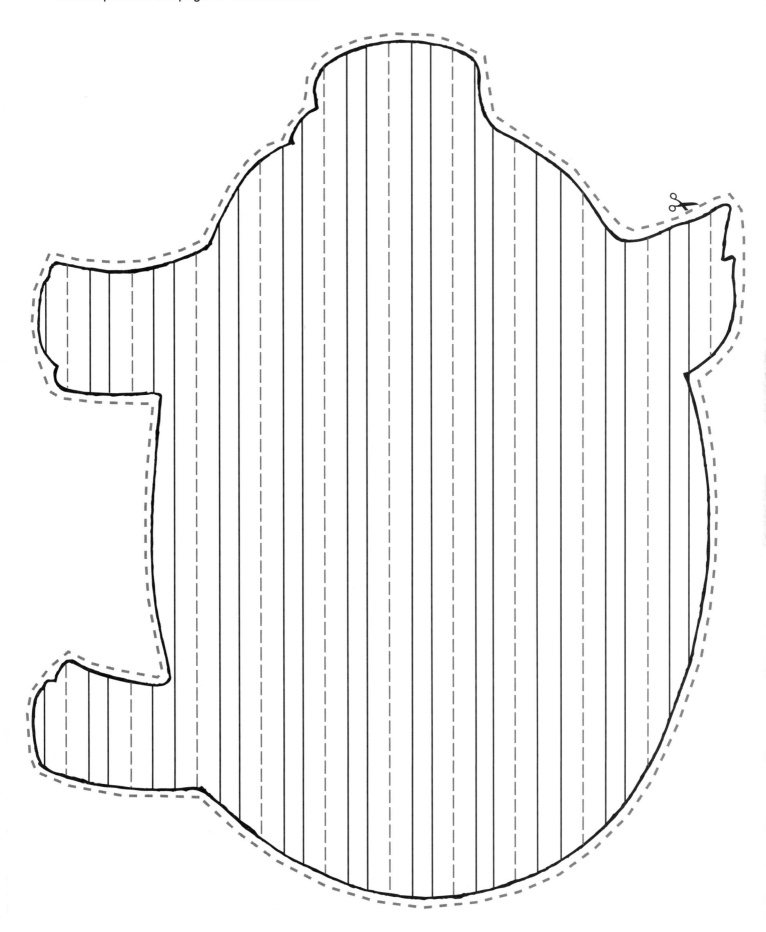

Note: Directions for using this clip art are on page 15.

pennies   nickels   dimes   quarters

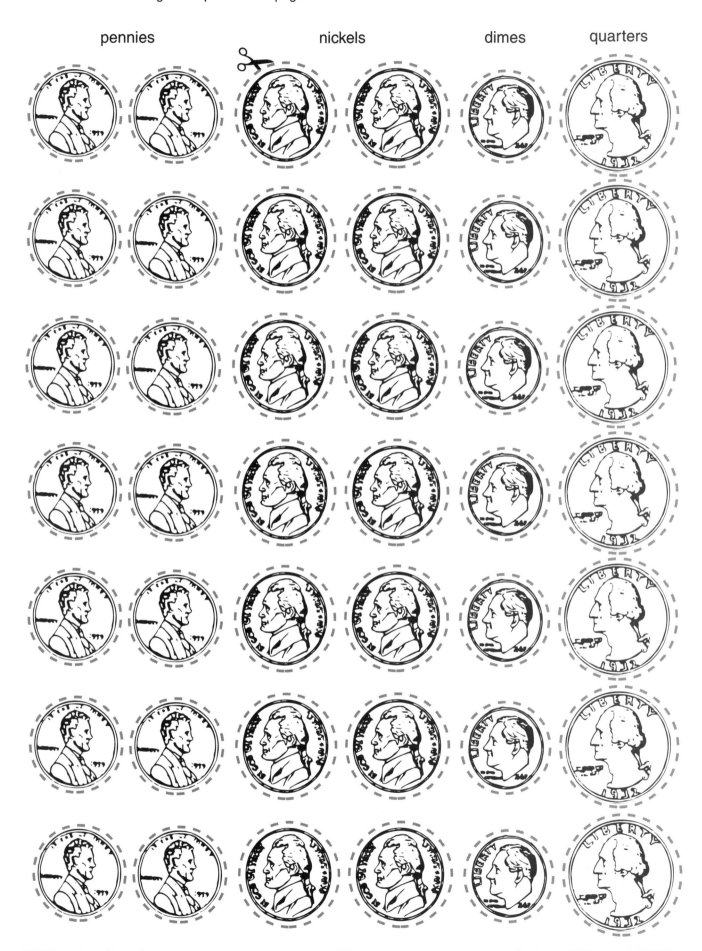

Doghouse

Prewriting Activities

Read

City Dog by Karla Kuskin; Clarion Books, 1998.
Any Kind of Dog by Lynn W. Reiser; Mulberry
  Books, 1994.
The Best Thing about a Puppy by Judy Hindley;
  Candlewick Press, 1998.
Arthur's New Puppy by Marc Tolon Brown; Little,
  Brown & Company, 1998.
All about Dogs and Puppies by Laura Driscoll
  & Wendy Cheyette Lewiston; Grosset &
  Dunlap, 1998.

Get Ready to Write

1. Brainstorm and list the names of different
   kinds of dogs. Then have students cut
   pictures of dogs from newspapers, magazines,
   and pet food packaging. Match the pictures to
   the names on the brainstorming list.

2. Discuss students' own dogs. What kinds do
   they have? What do their dogs look like?
   What can their dogs do? How do students
   take care of their dogs? Have them bring
   in photos of their dogs to share with the class.

Writing Activities

Individual Books

• Draw a Story

Reproduce the cover and several blank pages.
Help students think of their own topics for stories
or use one of the following ideas:

All Kinds of Dogs
Students draw a different kind of dog on each page.
Staple a cover to the pages.

I Take Care of My Dog
Students draw themselves caring for and playing with
a dog. Compile student pages and attach a cover.

• Complete the Sentences

Reproduce the cover, a blank form, and the cloze form.
Students complete the sentences to create a story and
then draw a picture on the blank form.

• Write a Story

Reproduce the cover and several lined forms. Students
write their own dog stories. Possible story starters:

How to Give a Dog a Bath   *My Pet Dog*
The Best Dog in the World   *Dog to the Rescue*
Little Lost Puppy   *Dexter, the Talking Dog*

cover

cloze form

lined form
for written
stories

Group Books

• Give Your Dog a Bone

Give each student a copy of the blank doghouse form and the
dog-bone clip art page. They are to draw a dog and a dog dish
inside the doghouse, write the name of the dog on the dish, and
paste one or more dog bones in the dish. Students who are ready
to write may want to add a sentence or two about their dogs.
Compile student pages and attach a cover.

• Dog Tricks

Give each student a copy of the blank doghouse form and one
or more lined forms. Brainstorm and list the kinds of tricks dogs
can do. Have students draw a dog doing a trick on the blank
form. Then have them write about the talented dog. Students
may describe the trick, explain how the dog learned to do the
trick, or create a story with the trick as an important part of
the plot. Compile student pages and attach a cover.

clip art

Note: Reproduce this book cover for each student.

23

Note: Reproduce this page to draw a picture story or to use as a back cover.

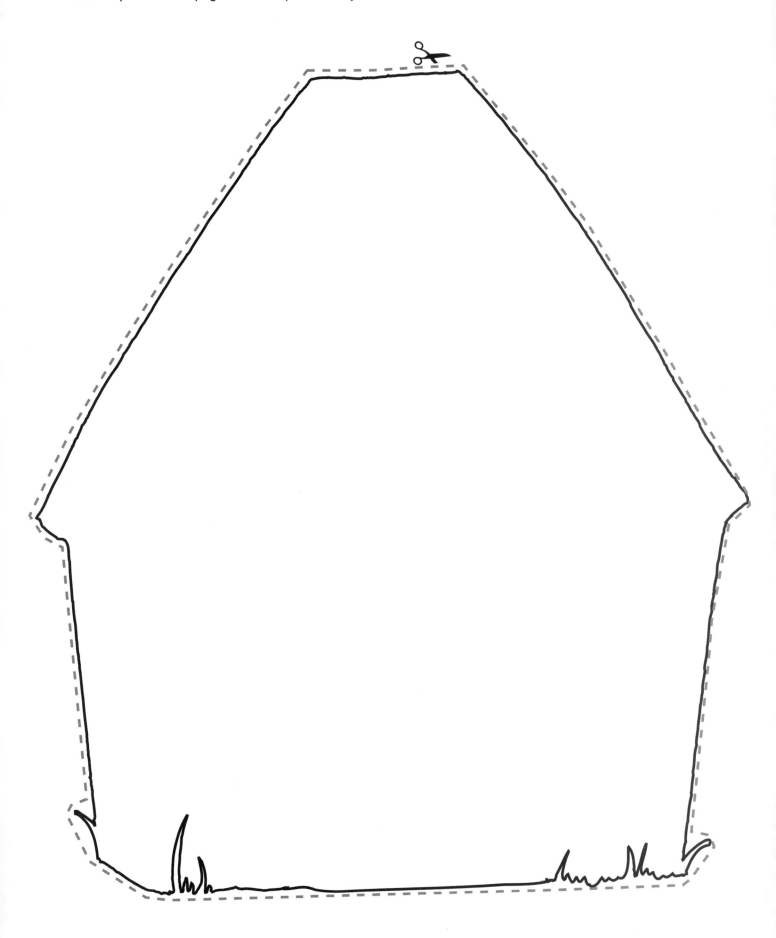

24

My Dog

by _____

See my _____ ,

_____ dog .

My dog can _____

_____ .

I take good care of my dog.

I _____

_____ .

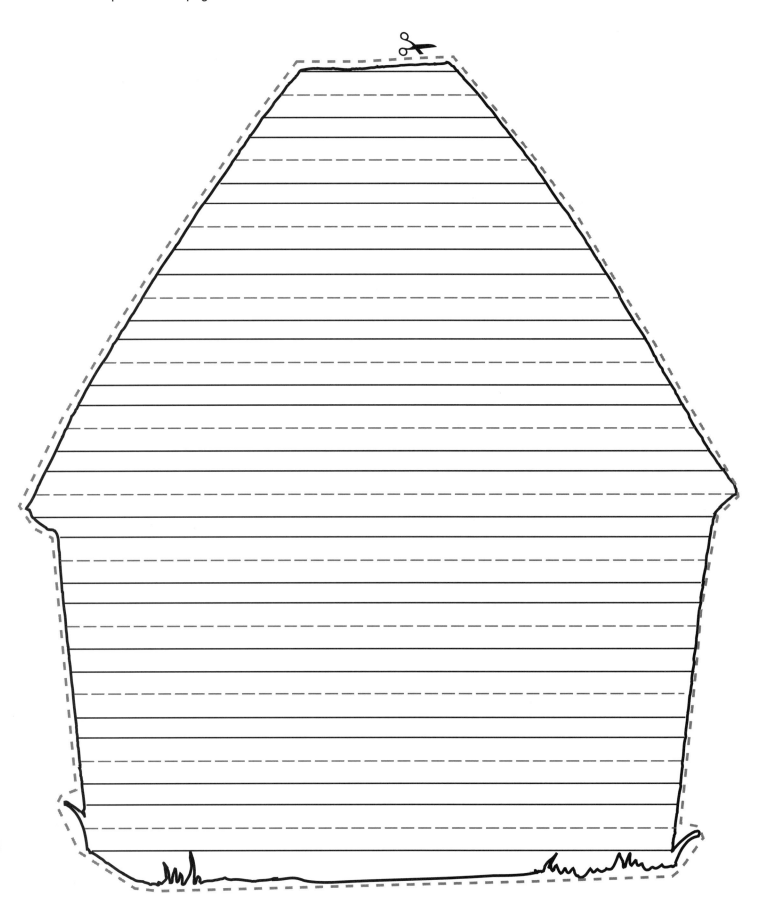

Beginning Writers • EMC 776

Note: Directions for using this clip art are on page 22.

Lunch Box

Prewriting Activities

Read

Lunch Boxes by Fred Ehrlich; Puffin, 1993.
Monster's Lunch Box by Marc Tolon Brown; Little, Brown and Company, 1995.
I Need a Lunch Box by Jeannette Caines; Harper & Row, 1993.
Halmoni and the Picnic by Sook Nyul Choi; Houghton Mifflin, 1993.

Get Ready to Write

1. Bring in a variety of types of lunch boxes or bags (metal, plastic, insulated, paper, etc.). Have students show the type of lunch box or bag they bring to school.

2. Brainstorm and list all of the kinds of food you might pack in your lunch box or bag. Discuss the kinds of covers, wrappings, or containers different types of foods need. Ask students to think of foods that should never be packed in a lunch box. Have them explain why.

Writing Activities

- **Draw a Story**
  Reproduce the cover and several blank pages.
  Help students think of their own topics for stories
  or use one of the following ideas:

  How to Make a Sandwich
  Students draw pictures to show the steps in making
  a sandwich.

  "_____'s Lunch"
  Students draw a different item they would like for lunch
  on each page (sandwich, fruit, cookie, drink, etc.).

- **Complete the Sentences**
  Reproduce the cover, a blank form, and the cloze form.
  Students complete the sentences to create a story and
  then draw a picture on the blank form.

- **Write a Story**
  Reproduce the cover and several lined forms. Students
  write their own lunch box stories. Possible story starters:

  How to Make a Sandwich   *My Favorite Lunch*
  Late for Lunch   *The Worst Lunch I Ever Ate*
  The Day I Forgot My Lunch   *The Magic Lunch Box*

cover

cloze form

lined form for written stories

Group Books

- **My Sandwich**
  Give each student a copy of the blank lunch box form and
  a bread slice from the clip art page. Talk about real and
  unusual sandwiches. Students are to color and cut out the
  bread, draw sandwich filling (real or unusual) on the bread
  slice, and paste it to the lunch box form. Then they are to list
  the ingredients that went on the slice of bread at the bottom
  of the page. Compile student pages and attach a cover.

- **A Surprise in My Lunch Box—A Riddle Book**
  Each student will need a lined lunch box form. Have students
  close their eyes and think of a nice surprise they might find
  in their lunch box. Have them share their ideas. Repeat the
  activity with students thinking about a funny surprise, and
  then a scary surprise. Students are to write a riddle about
  one surprise. Have them turn their page over and illustrate
  the surprise. Place the completed riddles and pictures in
  a cover. Classmates will read the riddle and then turn the
  page over to see the surprise.

peanut butter
grape jelly

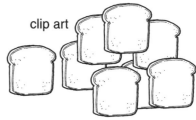

clip art

Note: Reproduce this book cover for each student.

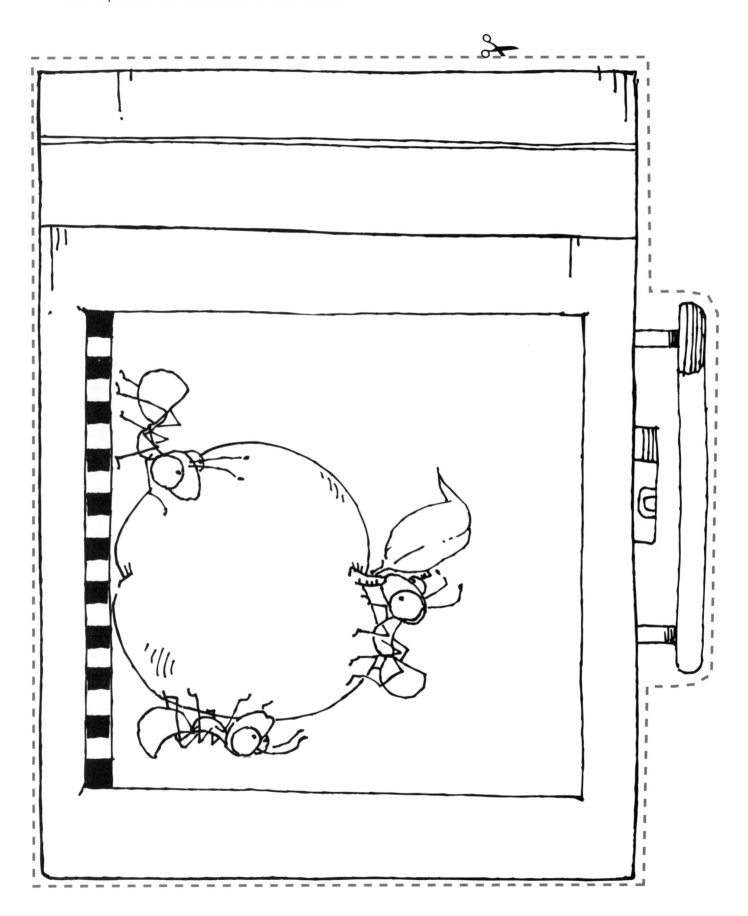

Note: Reproduce this page to draw a picture story or to use as a back cover.

Beginning Writers • EMC 776

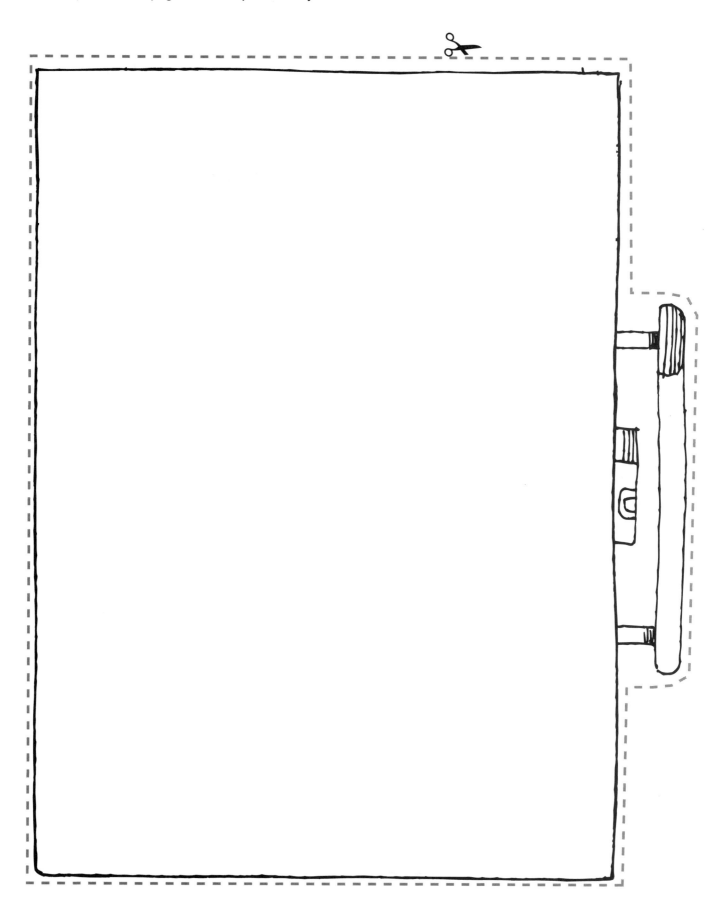

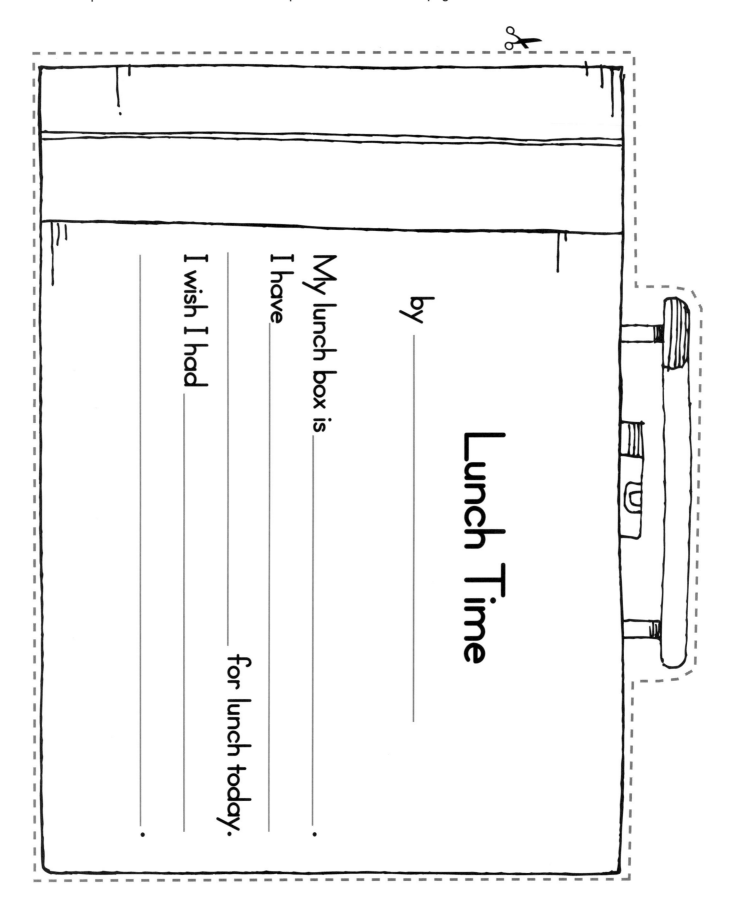

Lunch Time

by _____

My lunch box is _____ .

I have _____ for lunch today.

I wish I had _____ .

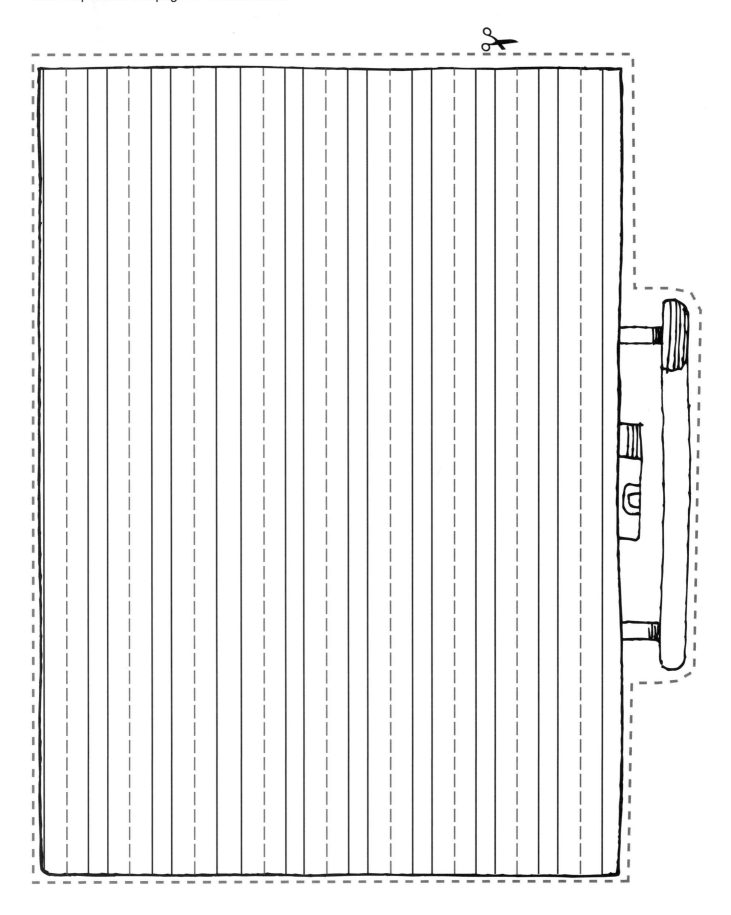

Pocket

Prewriting Activities

Read

Katy No Pocket by Emmy Payne; Sandpiper, 1973.

A Pocket for Corduroy by Don Freeman; Puffin, 1997.

Six Empty Pockets by Matt Curtis; Children's Press, 1997.

Pockets by Jennifer Armstrong; Crown Publishing, 1998.

Get Ready to Write

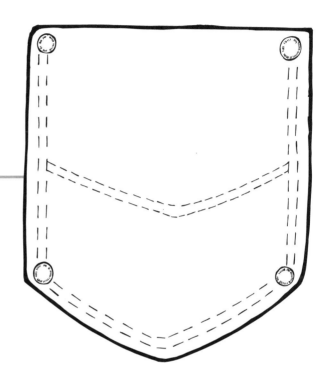

1. Discuss pockets and where they are found. Have students examine what they are wearing. How many pockets do they have? Where are the pockets? Have students describe their pockets (*small pocket on my vest; four pockets on my jeans; two big pockets on my jacket*). Extend the lesson by making a graph to show the number of students having a specific number (0 to 10 or more) of pockets.

2. Discuss the types of things we carry in our pockets. Have student volunteers empty their pockets. Make a list of the items they are carrying. Have students share the most unusual things they have ever carried in their pockets. Extend the discussion by naming other places we carry things (purse, wallet, coin purse, shoe, etc.).

Writing Activities

Individual Books

- **Draw a Story**
  Reproduce the cover and several blank pages.
  Help students think of their own topics for stories or use one of the following ideas:

  In _____'s Pocket
  Students draw an item on each pocket form that might be in the pocket of a person or character named (Dad's pocket, Teacher's pocket, Big Bad Wolf's pocket, etc.).

  All Kinds of Pockets
  Students draw a different type of pocket on each page (on jeans, on a jacket, on a kangaroo, on a carpenter's apron, etc.).

- **Complete the Sentences**
  Reproduce the cover, a blank form, and the cloze form. Students complete the sentences to create a story and then draw a picture on the blank form.

- **Write a Story**
  Reproduce the cover and several lined forms. Students write their own pocket stories. Possible story starters:

A Hole in My Pocket	*In a Circus Clown's Pocket*
My Secret Pocket	*A Surprise in My Pocket*
No Pockets	*In _____'s Pocket*

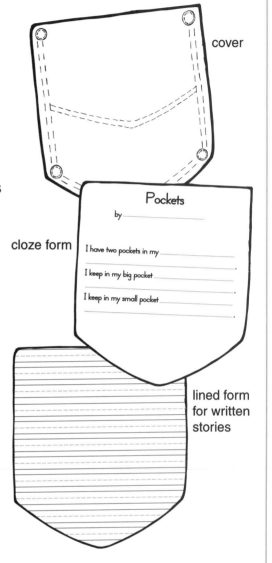

cover

cloze form

Pockets

by _____

I have two pockets in my _____

I keep in my big pocket _____

I keep in my small pocket _____

lined form for written stories

Group Books

- **What Is in My Pocket?—A Riddle Book**
  Give each student a copy of the blank pocket form and a copy of the lined form. They may choose an object from page 41 to paste to the blank form or draw something of their own. Have students write a short riddle about that object on the lined form. Staple the riddles and answers together in a cover, being sure each riddle page comes before its answer.

- **"Starts Like Pocket"**
  Give each student a copy of the blank pocket form. Brainstorm and list items that begin with the sound /p/. Have students draw an object on the form and write a phrase naming what is in the pocket (*a penny in my pocket, a pickle in my pocket, a pencil in my pocket, a parrot in my pocket, etc.*).

I am a frog.

clip art

Note: Reproduce this book cover for each student.

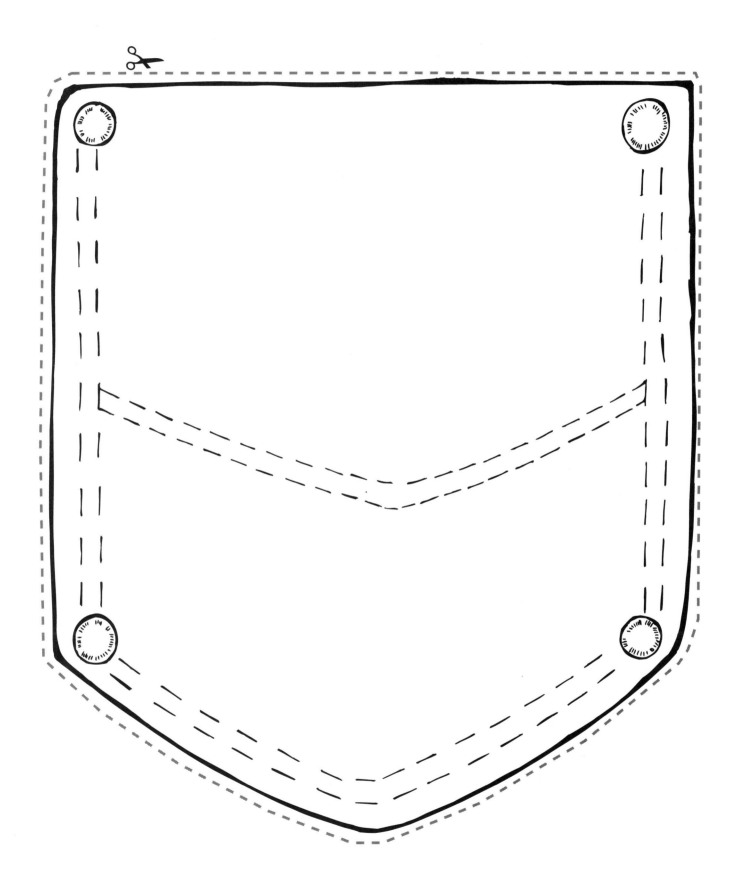

Note: Reproduce this page to draw a picture story or to use as a back cover.

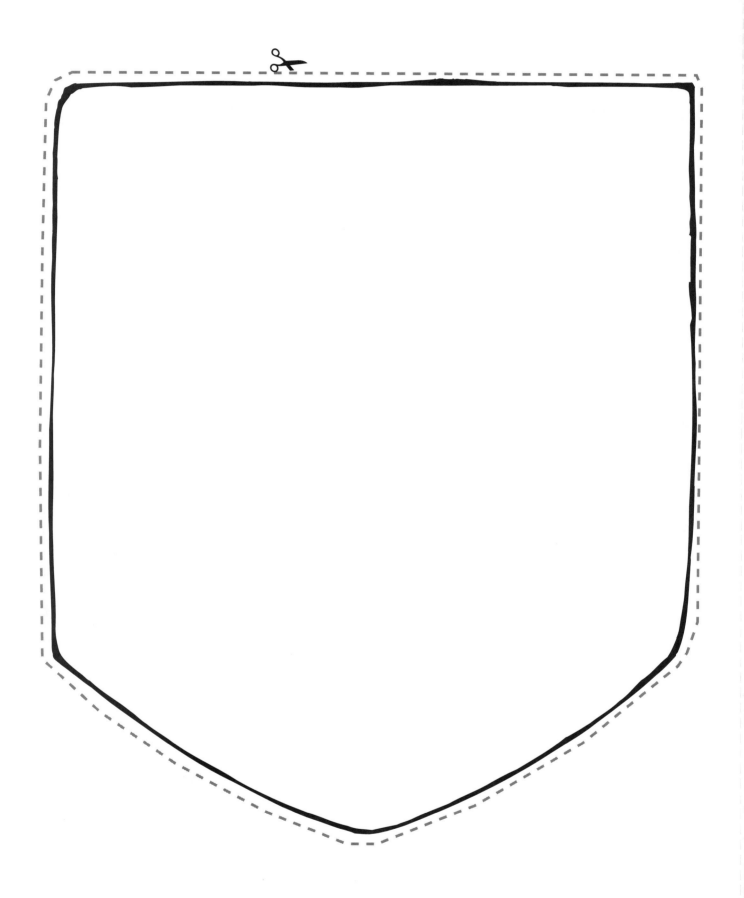

Pockets

by _____

I have two pockets in my _____ .

I keep _____ in my big pocket.

I keep _____ in my small pocket.

Beginning Writers • EMC 776

Note: Reproduce this page for written stories.

Beginning Writers • EMC 776

Note: Directions for using this clip art are on page 36.

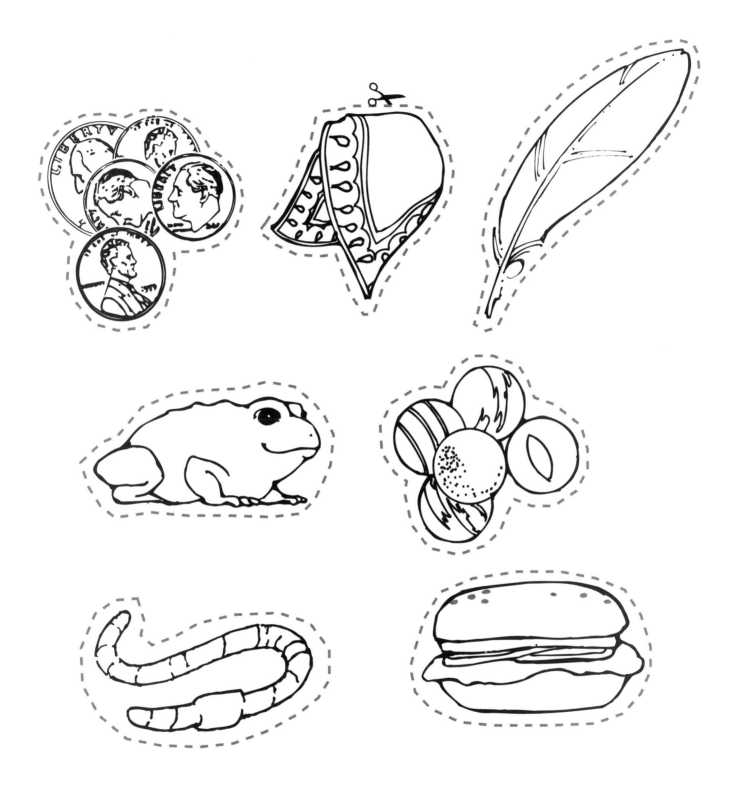

Fishbowl

Prewriting Activities

Read

Little Fish Lost by Nancy Van Laan; Atheneum, 1998.

Amazing Fish (Eyewitness Juniors) by Mary Ling; Knopf, 1991.

Fish Story by Katherine Andres; Simon and Schuster, 1993.

Fish Eyes: A Book You Can Count On by Lois Ehlert; Harcourt Brace, 1992.

The Fisherman and His Wife by Rosemary Wells; Dial Books for Young Readers, 1998.

A Million Fish...More or Less by Patricia C. McKissack; Dragonfly, 1996.

Get Ready to Write

1. Set up a fishbowl in the classroom. Include a fish, some rocks or sand, small plants, and a water snail. Use the fishbowl to develop vocabulary about how fish behave (swim, eat, dive, breathe, etc.) and what they need.

2. Collect pictures of different types of fish. Use the pictures for comparing and contrasting fish. This is another excellent way to increase vocabulary.

Writing Activities

Individual Books

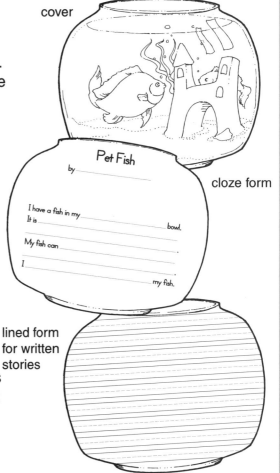

cover

cloze form

lined form
for written
stories

- **Draw a Story**
Reproduce the cover and several blank fishbowl pages.
Help students think of their own topics for stories or use
one of the following ideas:

  Colorful Fish
  Students draw a fish on each page using a different
  color and pattern. Students dictate or write the word
  for the color used on the page.

  My Pet Fish
  Students draw a different picture on each page
  showing how to take care of a pet fish.

- **Complete the Sentences**
Reproduce the cover, a blank fishbowl form, and the
cloze form. Students complete the sentences to create
a story and then draw a picture on the blank form.

- **Write a Story**
Reproduce the cover and several lined forms. Students
write their own fishbowl stories. Possible story starters:

Big Fish, Little Fish	*A Strange Fish in My Bowl*
A Birthday Surprise	*Watch Out for That Cat!*
One Fish in a Dish	*If I Lived in a Fishbowl*

Group Books

- **A Rainbow Fish Book**
Give each student a blank fishbowl form and three fish from
page 48. Assign a color of the rainbow to each student. Each
student is make an interesting pattern on the fish using only
the assigned color. Then have students cut out the fish and
paste it in the fishbowl. Compile student pages in the order
the colors appear in a rainbow (red, orange, yellow, green,
blue, indigo, violet) and attach a cover.

- **"Make A Wish," Said the Fish**
Give each student a 9" x 12" (23 x 30.5 cm) sheet of blue
construction paper, a fish from the clip art page, and the
lined form. Read a version of *The Fisherman and His Wife*
to the class. Have students think about what they would ask for if they discovered a magic
fish in their fishbowl. Have students write their wishes on the lined form. Then cut out the
fishbowl form and paste it to the construction paper. Then have students cut out the fish
and paste it above the bowl to look like it has jumped out. Have students draw a speech
bubble near the fish and write "Make a wish." Compile student pages and add a cover.

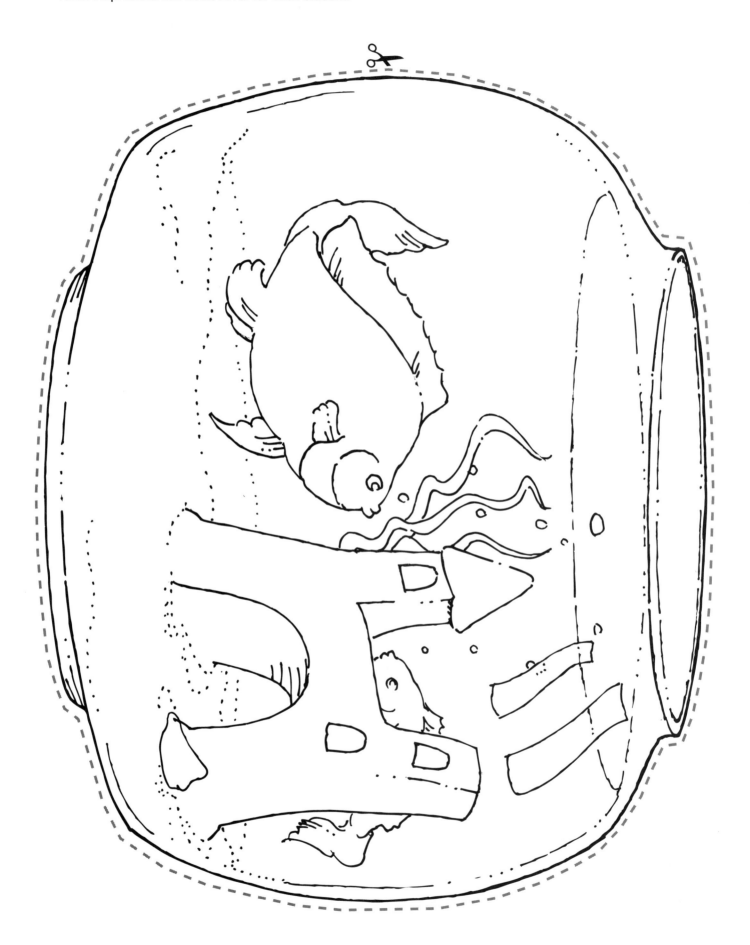

Note: Reproduce this page to draw a picture story or to use as a back cover.

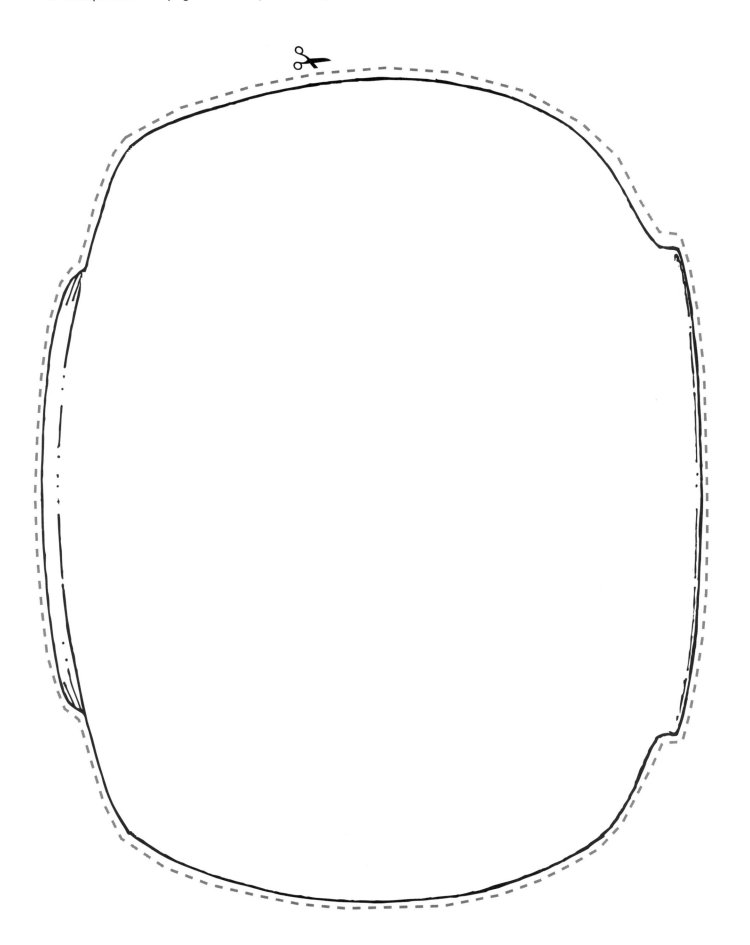

Beginning Writers • EMC 776

Note: Reproduce this form to use with Complete the Sentences on page 43.

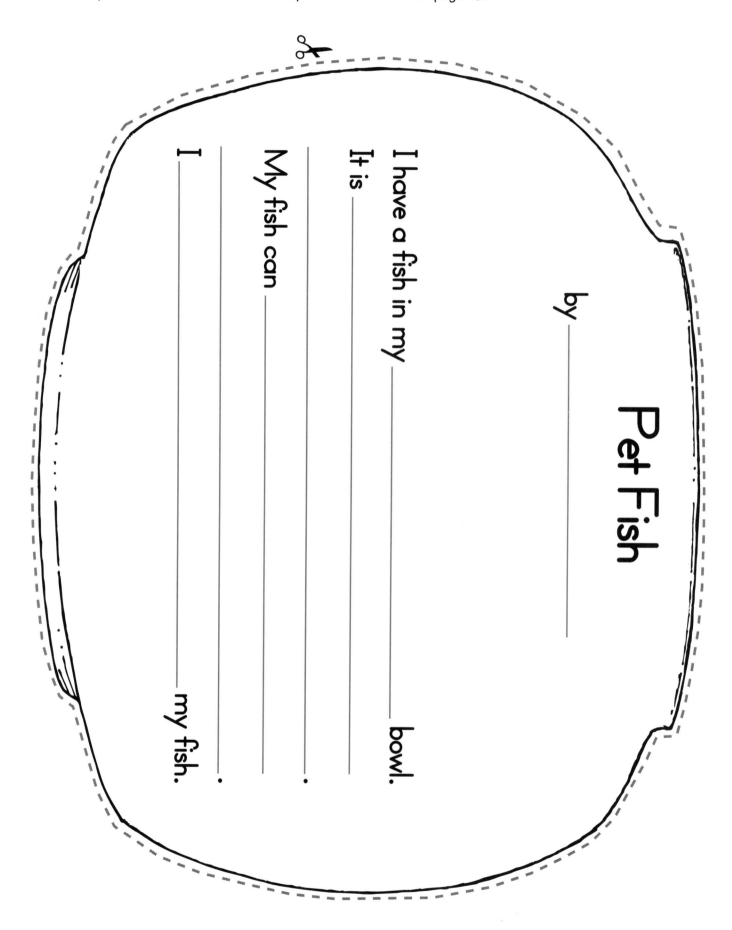

Pet Fish

by _____

I have a fish in my _____

It is _____

My fish can _____

I _____ my fish.

       Beginning Writers • EMC 776

Note: Reproduce this page for written stories.

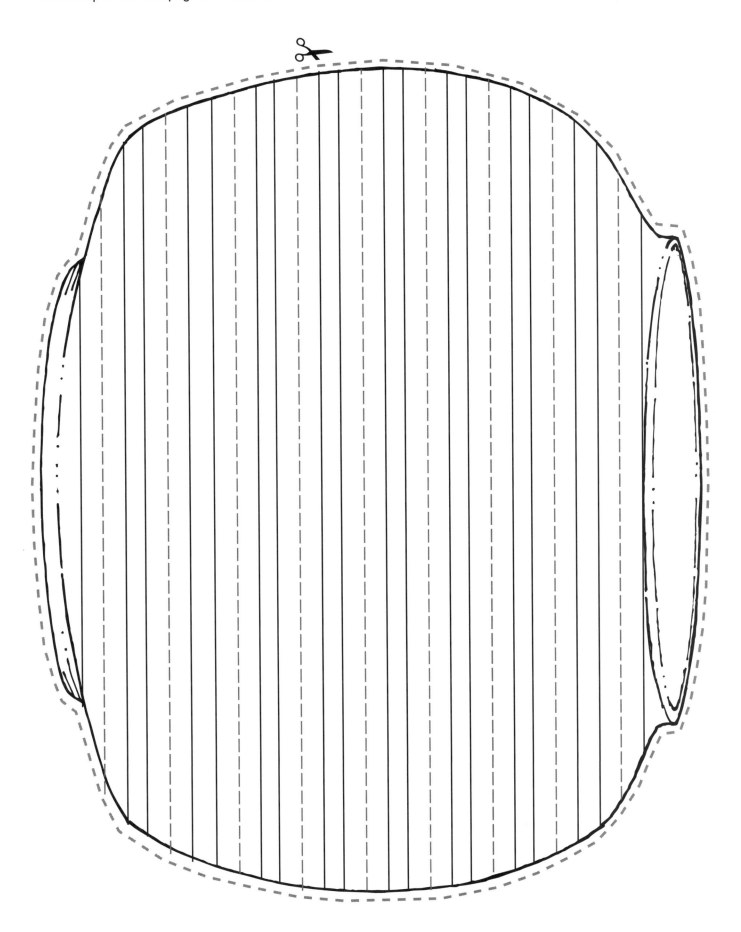

Beginning Writers • EMC 776

Note: Directions for using this clip art are on page 43.

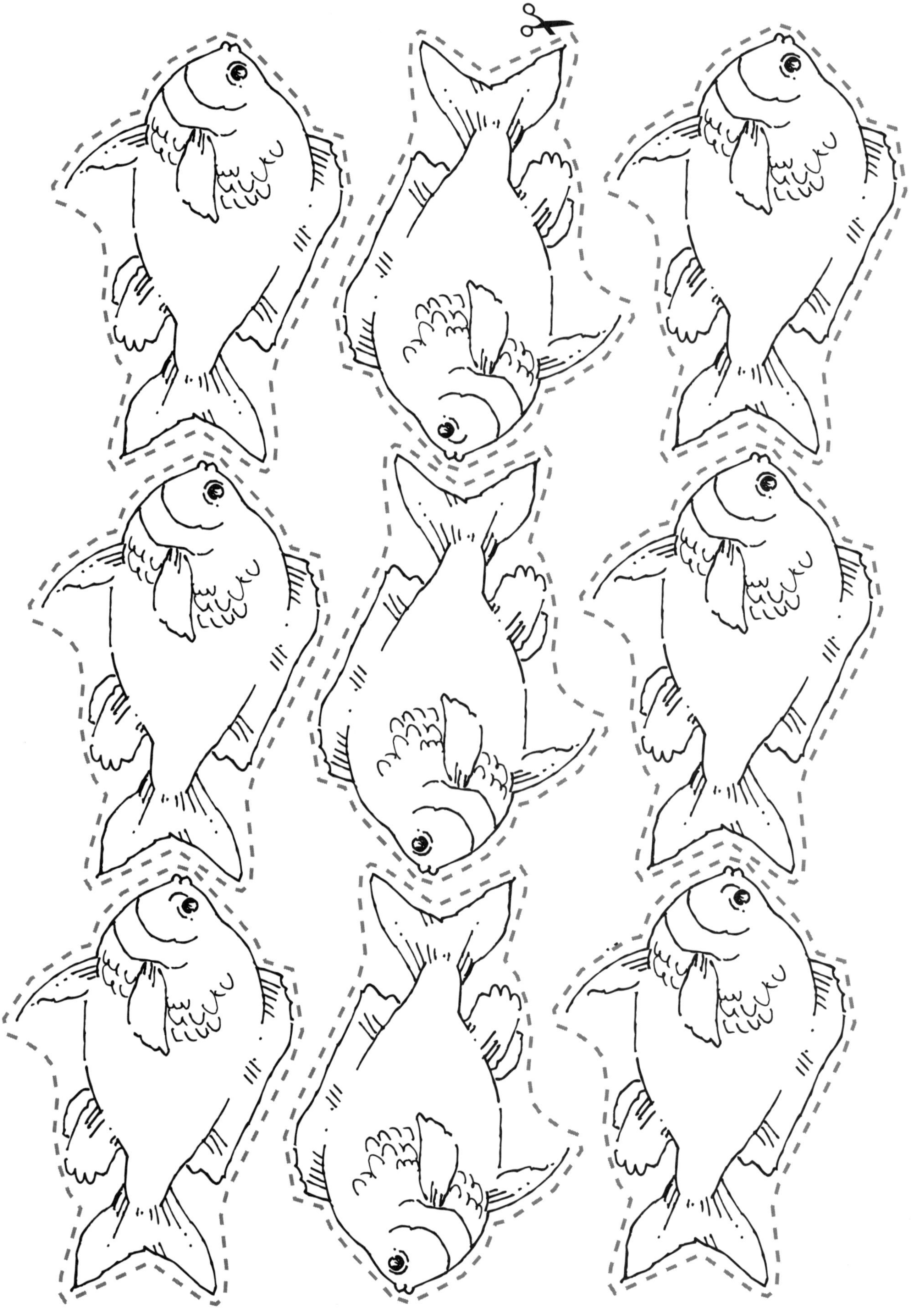

Circus Tent

Prewriting Activities

Read

Babar's Little Circus Star by Laurent de Brunhoff;
  Random House, 1988.
Englebert Joins the Circus by Tom Paxton;
  William Morrow and Company, 1997.
Clifford at the Circus by Norman Bridwell;
  Scholastic Trade, 1990.
Peter Spier's Circus by Peter Spier;
  Yearling Books, 1995.
Circus by Jack Prelutsky; Aladdin
  Paperbacks, 1989.
Backyard Big Top by Jill Kastner; Simon
  & Schuster, 1997.

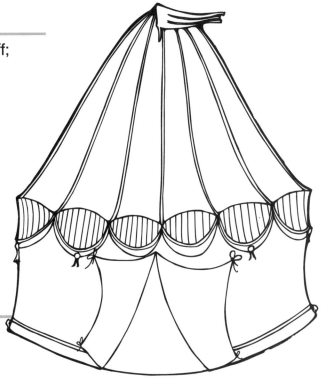

Get Ready to Write

1. Share a book about the circus. Discuss the animals, objects, and people found in a circus. Talk about the costumes the people wear and the kinds of acts the animals and people perform.

2. Guide students to act out different circus animal movements, sounds, and tricks. Call on volunteers to act out the action or sound of one of the circus animals. The rest of the class tries to guess the animal's name. Complete the activity by playing circus music as students march around the classroom as circus animals to create a "Circus Parade."

 Beginning Writers • EMC 776

Writing Activities

Individual Books

- **Draw a Story**

  Reproduce the cover and several blank pages.
  Help students think of their own topics for stories
  or use one of the following ideas:

  People in the Circus
  Students draw a different circus performer
  on each page.

  A Trip to the Circus
  Students draw a different scene on each
  page to show a family trip to the circus.

- **Complete the Sentences**

  Reproduce the cover, a blank form, and the cloze form.
  Students complete the sentences to create a story and
  then draw a picture on the blank form.

- **Write a Story**

  Reproduce the cover and several lined forms. Students
  write their own circus stories. Possible story starters:

Be a Clown	*Funny Clowns*
The Lion Tamer	*Elephant Tricks*
Under the Big Tent	*When I Was in the Circus*

cover

Circus Fun
by _____

I went to the circus with _____.
I saw a clown _____.
I saw _____.

cloze form

lined form
for written
stories

Group Books

- **Where's the Clown?—Positional Words**

  Give each student the blank circus tent form, a lined form,
  and a clown, ball, and dog from the circus clip art on page 55.
  Students will color, cut out, and paste the three pictures to the
  blank page. They will then write or dictate sentences using
  positional words to describe where things are in the pictures.
  (*The clown is behind the little puppy. The red ball is over the
  clown's head. The funny clown is standing on the ball.*) Staple
  the pages together with a cover.

- **Juggling Clowns—A Counting Book**

  Give each student a copy of the blank circus tent. Each student
  will need a clown and up to 10 balls from the clip art on page 55.
  Assign each student a number between 1 and 10. Students color,
  cut out, and paste a clown to the blank form. They then color, cut
  out, and paste balls arranged as if the clown is juggling them. Students
  write a sentence telling how many balls are on the page. (*My clown
  can juggle three balls.*) Compile student pages and attach a cover.

The dog is on the ball.

clip art

Note: Reproduce this book cover for each student.

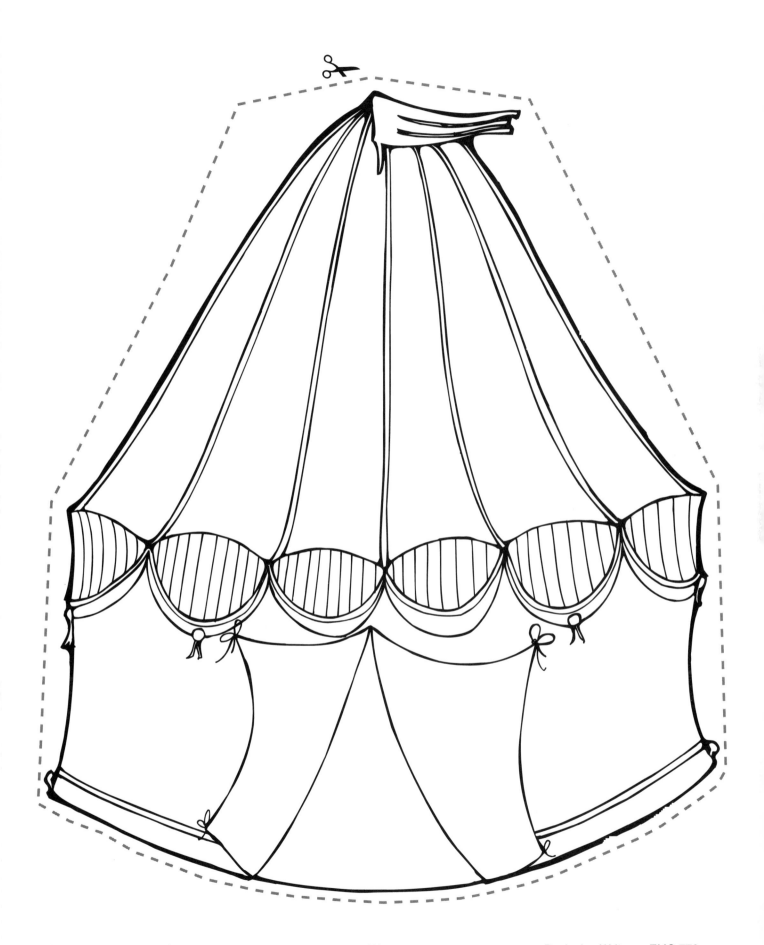

51

Note: Reproduce this page to draw a picture story or to use as a back cover.

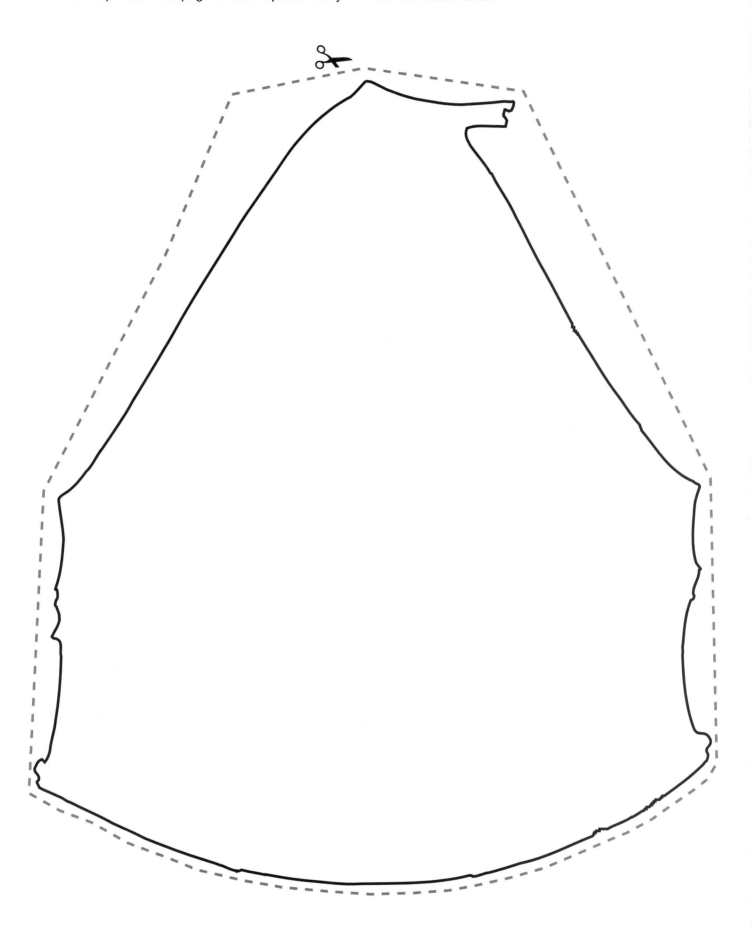

Beginning Writers • EMC 776

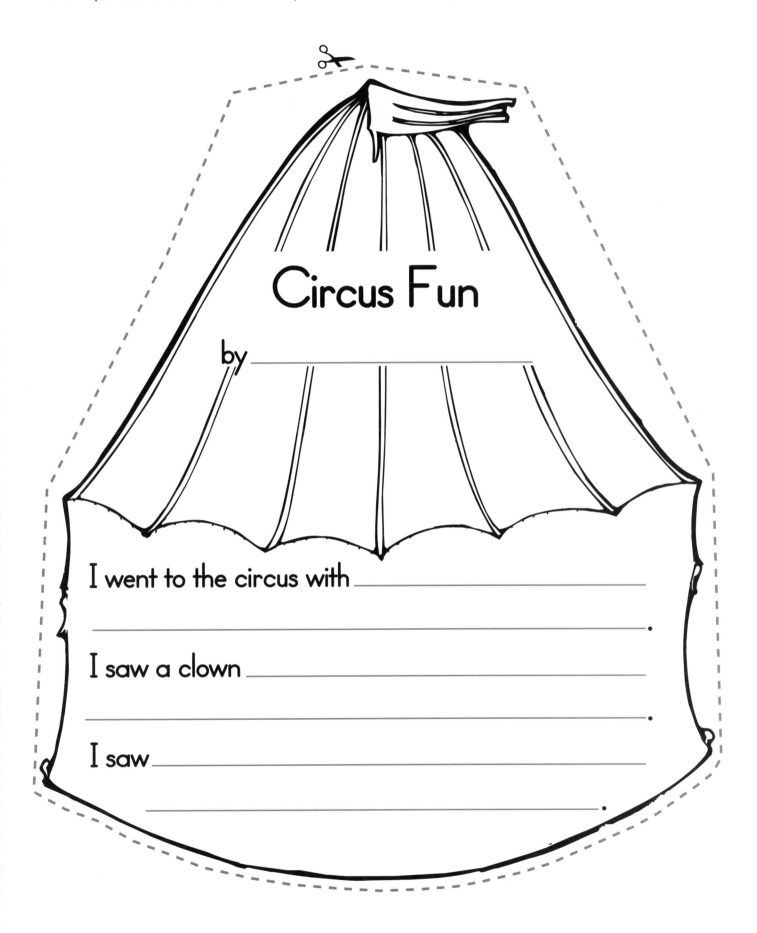

Circus Fun

by _____

I went to the circus with _____

_____.

I saw a clown _____

_____.

I saw _____

_____.

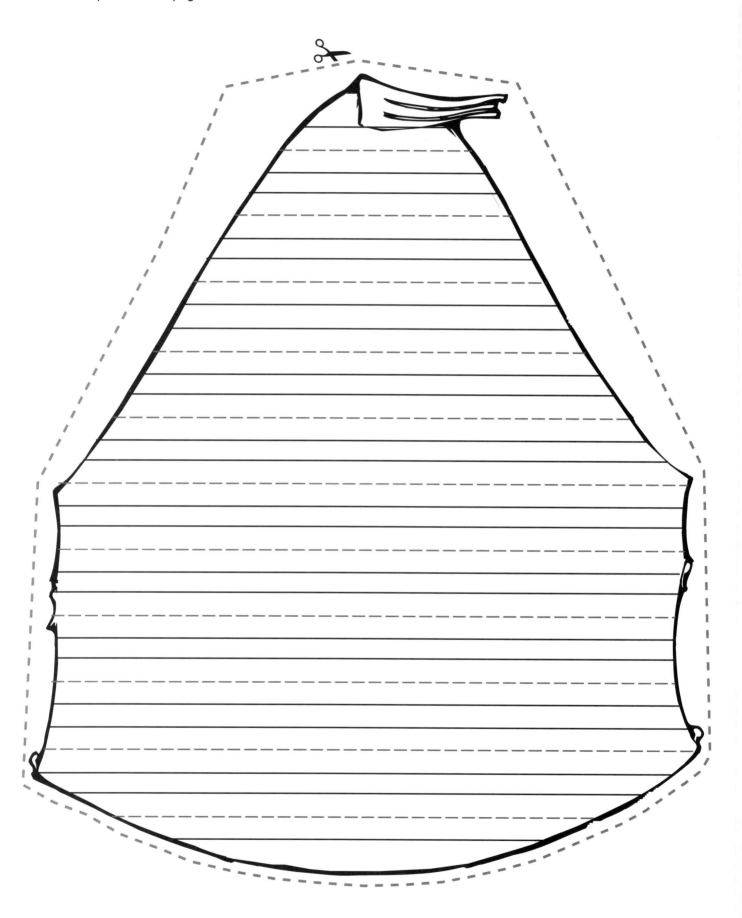

Note: Directions for using this clip art are on page 50.

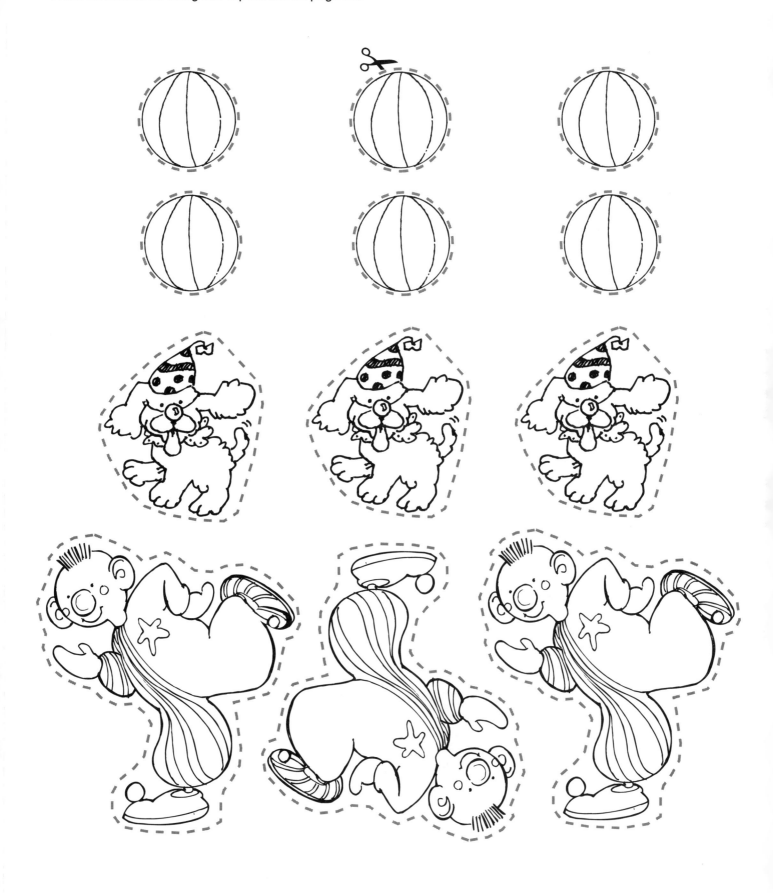

Duck

Prewriting Activities

Read

The Story about Ping by Marjorie Flack; Viking
   Press, 1977.
Across the Stream by Mirra Ginsburg;
   Mulberry Books, 1991.
Ducks Like to Swim by Agnes Verbover;
   Orchard Books, 1997.
Come Along, Daisy! by Jane Simmons;
   Little, Brown & Company, 1998.
Chibi: A True Story from Japan by Barbara
   Brenner; Clarion Books, 1996.
The Tale of Jemima Puddle-Duck by Beatrix
   Potter; Puffin, 1992.
Make Way for Ducklings by Robert
   McCloskey; Viking Press, 1941.

Get Ready to Write

1. Brainstorm and find out what your students
   know about ducks. What do ducks look like?
   Where do they live? What can they do?

2. Baby ducks are called ducklings. Discuss
   the names of other birds and their babies,
   (hen/chick, goose/gosling, swan/cygnet, etc.).
   You may want to extend the discussion to
   include names of other types of animal babies.

Writing Activities

Individual Books

• **Draw a Story**

Reproduce the cover and several blank pages.
Help students think of their own topics for stories
or use one of the following ideas:

Ducklings
Give each student three duckling patterns from page 62.
They are to paste one duckling on each blank form, and
then draw a background showing what each duckling is doing.

On the Farm
Discuss the different activities of a duck (eating, waddling
across the barnyard, swimming, etc.) Have students
draw a story showing a duck living on a farm.

• **Complete the Sentences**

Reproduce the cover, a blank form, and the cloze form.
Students complete the sentences to create a story and
then draw a picture on the blank form.

• **Write a Story**

Reproduce the cover and several lined forms. Students
write their own duck stories. Possible story starters:

Ducks at the Pond	*Ducks on a Farm*
Mother Duck and Her Ducklings	*Little Yellow Ducklings*
Learning to Swim	*Quack!*

cover

cloze form

lined form
for written
stories

Group Books

• **D Is for Duck**

Reproduce the blank pond form and one duck from page 62
for each student. They will color and cut out the duck and paste
it to the blank page. Students then add a drawing of another
item beginning with the sound of the letter /d/. Finally, students
dictate or write a phrase describing what is on the page
(*a duck in a dish, a duck eating doughnuts, a duck wearing
a dress, a duck dancing*). Compile student pages and attach
a cover.

• **Animal Mothers and Babies**

Brainstorm and create a list of animal mothers and their babies.
(Read *A Pinky Is a Baby Mouse* by Pam Muñoz Ryan; Hyperion Books
for Children, 1997.) Paste a duckling and the duck on the cover. Give
blank forms to students. Have students draw an animal mother and her baby,
and write what each is called. Compile student pages and attach the cover.

a duck wearing
a dress

Note: Reproduce this book cover for each student.

58

Note: Reproduce this page to draw a picture story or to use as a back cover.

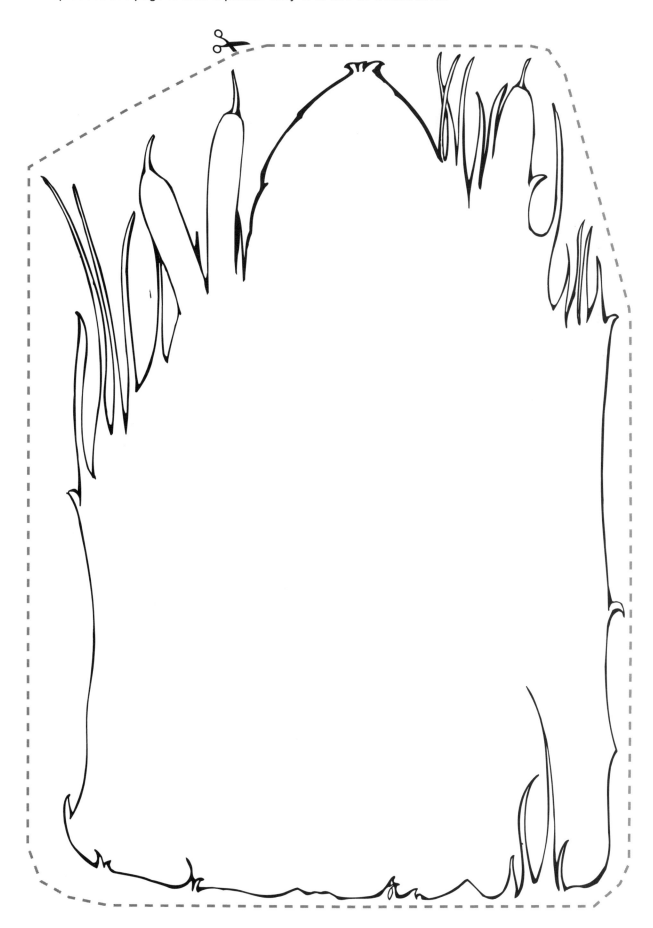

Beginning Writers • EMC 776

Mother Duck

by _____

See the big duck.

She is _____.

She has _____ little ducklings.

Her ducklings are _____

_____.

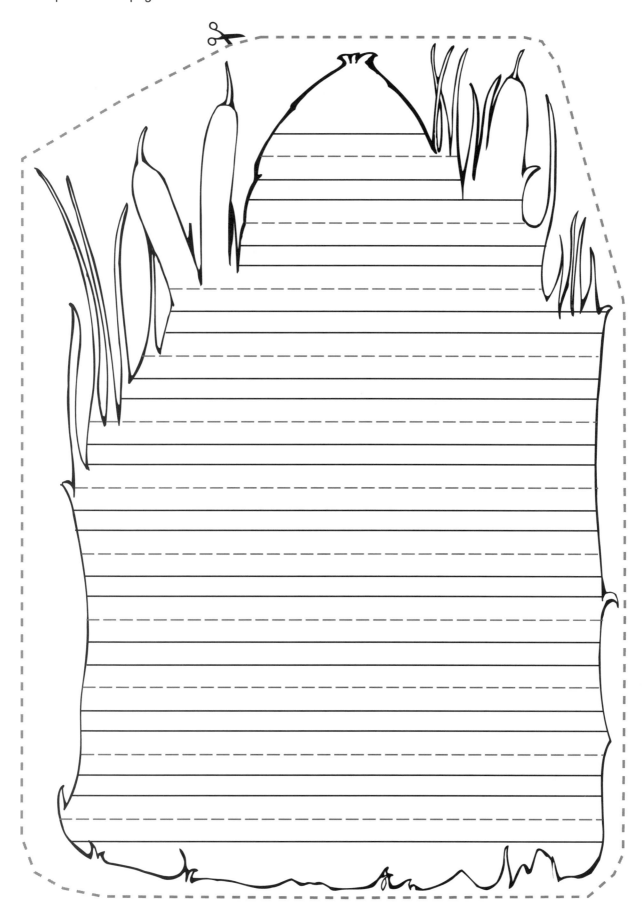

Note: Directions for using this clip art are on page 57.

Beginning Writers • EMC 776

Prewriting Activities

Read

Hamster by Barrie Watts; Silver Burdett Press, 1987.

Me and My Pet Rabbit by Christine Morley and Carole Orbell; World Book Inc., 1997.

Your Pet Gerbil by Elaine Landau; Children's Press, 1997.

I Love Guinea Pigs by Dick King-Smith; Candlewick Press, 1997.

A Look through the Mouse Hole by Heiderose Fisher-Nagel and Andreas Fisher-Nagel; Carolrhoda Books, 1989.

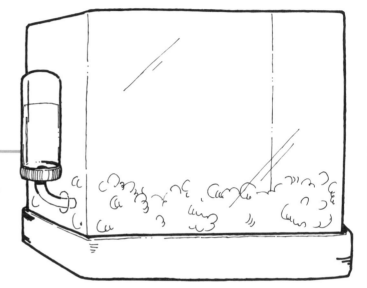

Get Ready to Write

1. Bring in one or more pets in cages (hamster, guinea pig, mouse, rat, rabbit). Have students name and describe the animal, the parts of its cage, and the equipment needed to care for the pet. Discuss the best way to care for the pet to keep it healthy and happy.

2. Brainstorm and list all of the kinds of pets you might keep in a cage in the classroom. Have students decide which of the small animals they would like to have in class if they could have only one. Graph the results.

Writing Activities

Individual Books

- **Draw a Story**
  Reproduce the cover and several blank pages.
  Help students think of their own topics for stories
  or use one of the following ideas:

  Little Pets
  Students draw a different pet on each blank
  cage form.

  My Pet
  Students draw a pet in action. Some students
  may want to write or dictate a phrase or sentence
  describing the action.

- **Complete the Sentences**
  Reproduce the cover, a blank form, and the cloze form.
  Students complete the sentences to create a story and
  then draw a picture on the blank form.

- **Write a Story**
  Reproduce the cover and several lined forms. Students
  write their own pet-in-a-cage stories. Possible story starters:

The Most Unusual Pet	*How I Take Care of My Pet*
Hamster Habits	*The Rabbit's Surprise*
A Trip to the Pet Store	*Mice Are Nice!*

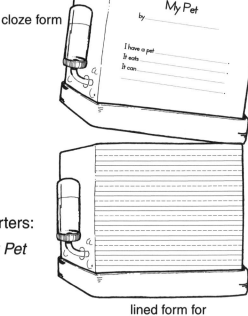

cover

cloze form

lined form for
written stories

Group Books

- **My Pet**
  Give each student a blank pet cage form and the animal clip
  art on page 69. They are to choose one of the animals to
  paste to the blank form or to draw an animal of their own.
  At the bottom of the page, students will write or dictate
  a descriptive phrase using at least two describing words
  *(a fat, fluffy hamster; a black, furry bunny; my little white
  mouse with pink eyes and a long, scaly tail).* Compile
  student pages and attach a cover.

- **The Day My Pet Escaped**
  Each student will need one or more lined forms. They
  are to write about where they found the "escapee" and
  how they caught it. Compile student pages and attach
  a cover.

clip art

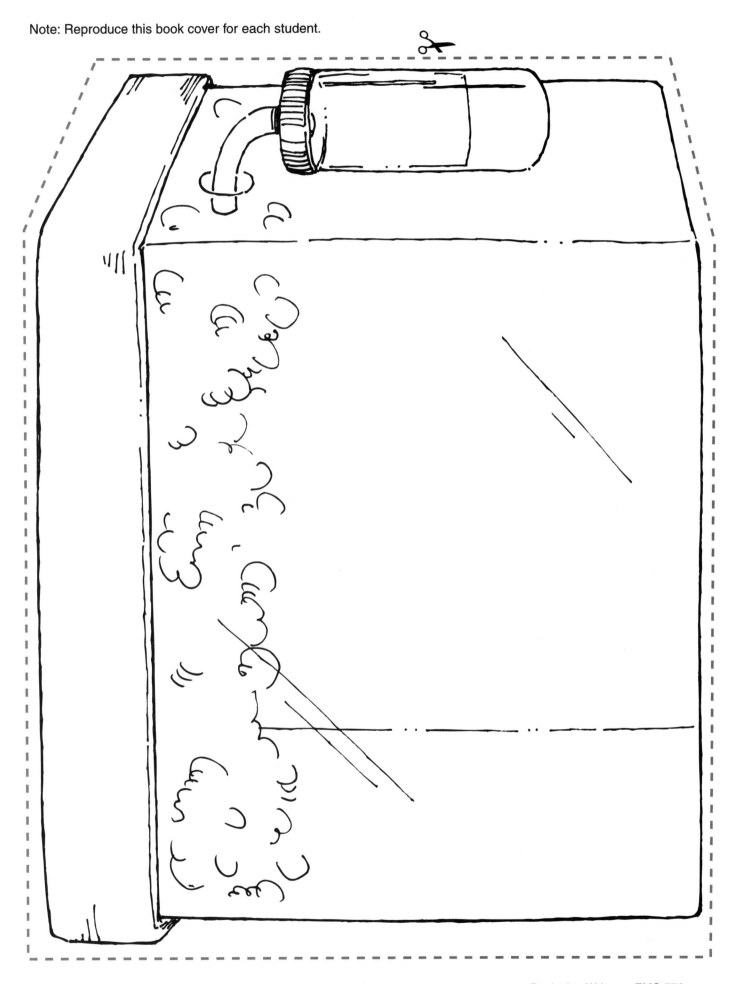

Note: Reproduce this page to draw a picture story or to use as a back cover.

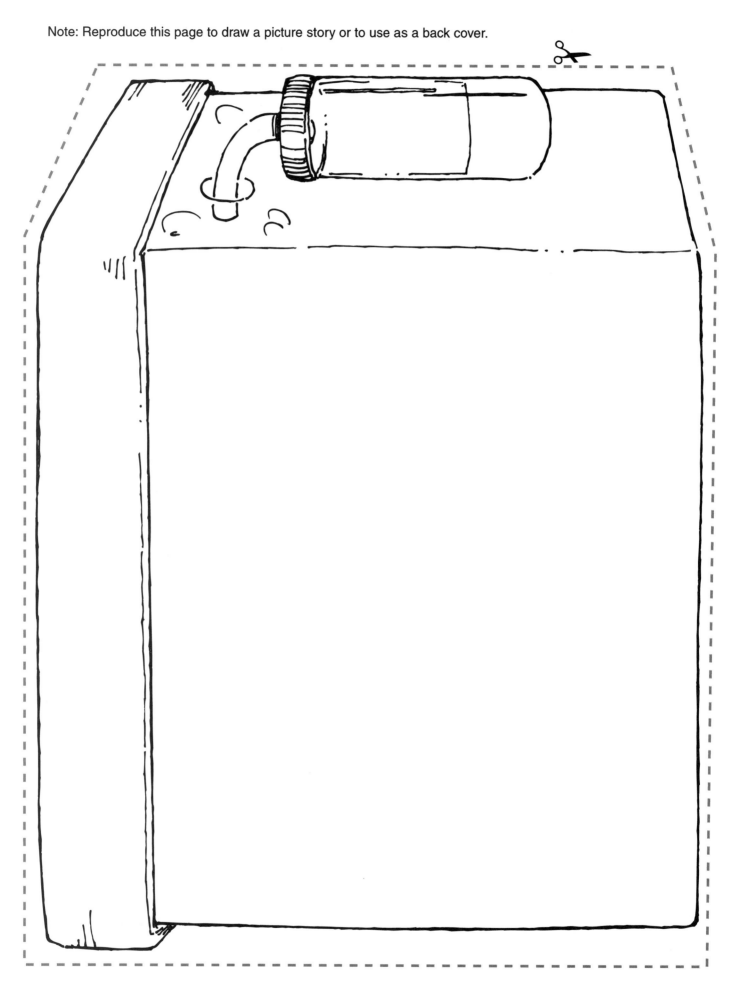

Beginning Writers • EMC 776

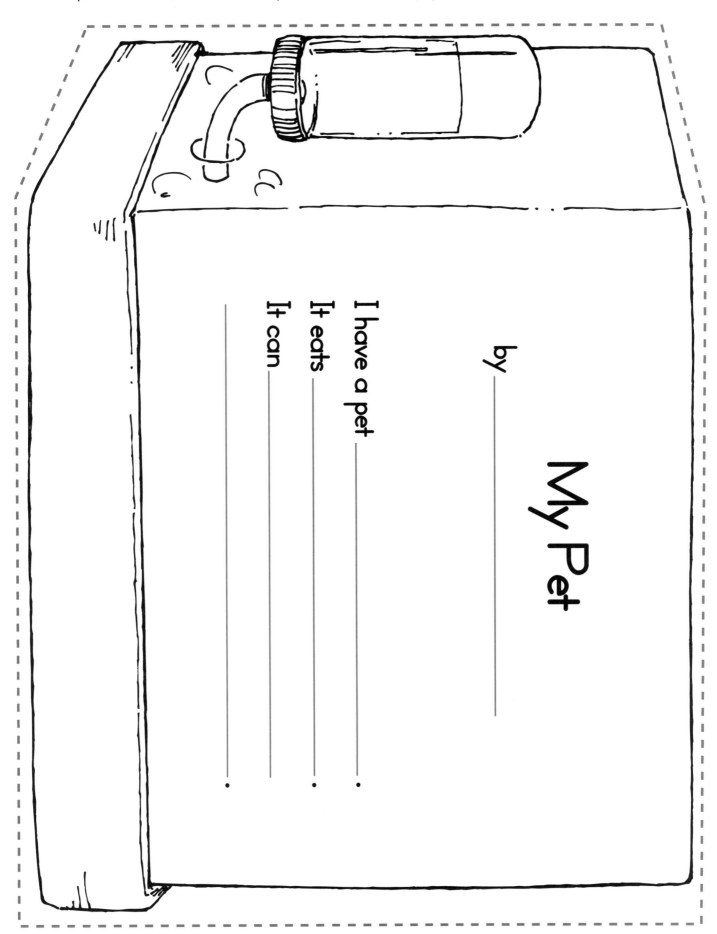

My Pet

by _____

I have a pet _____

It eats _____

It can _____

_____

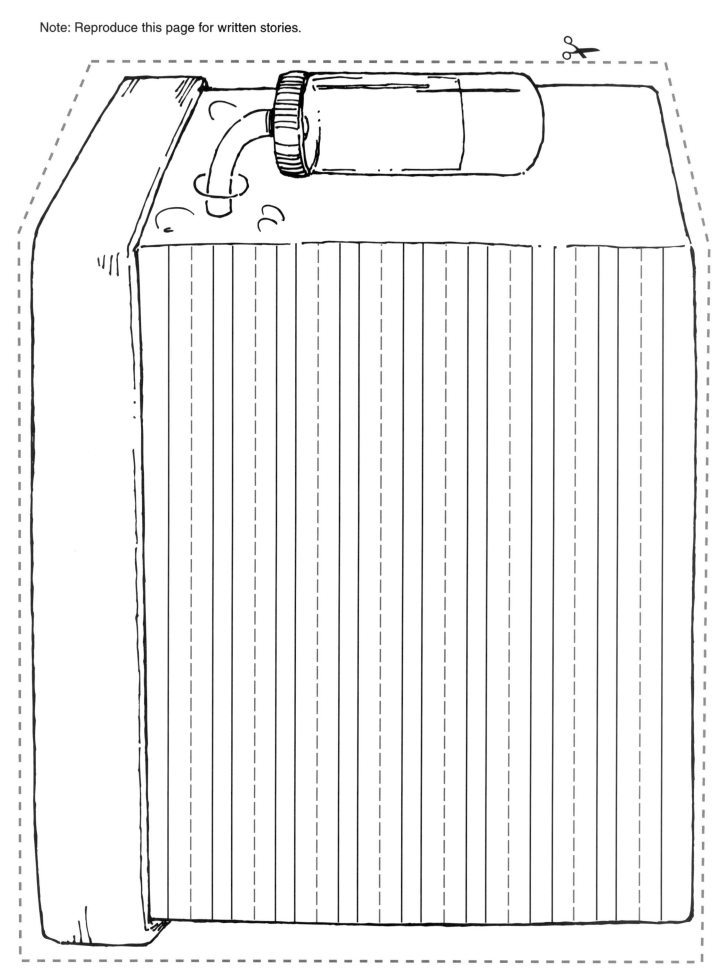

68

Note: Directions for using this clip art are on page 64.

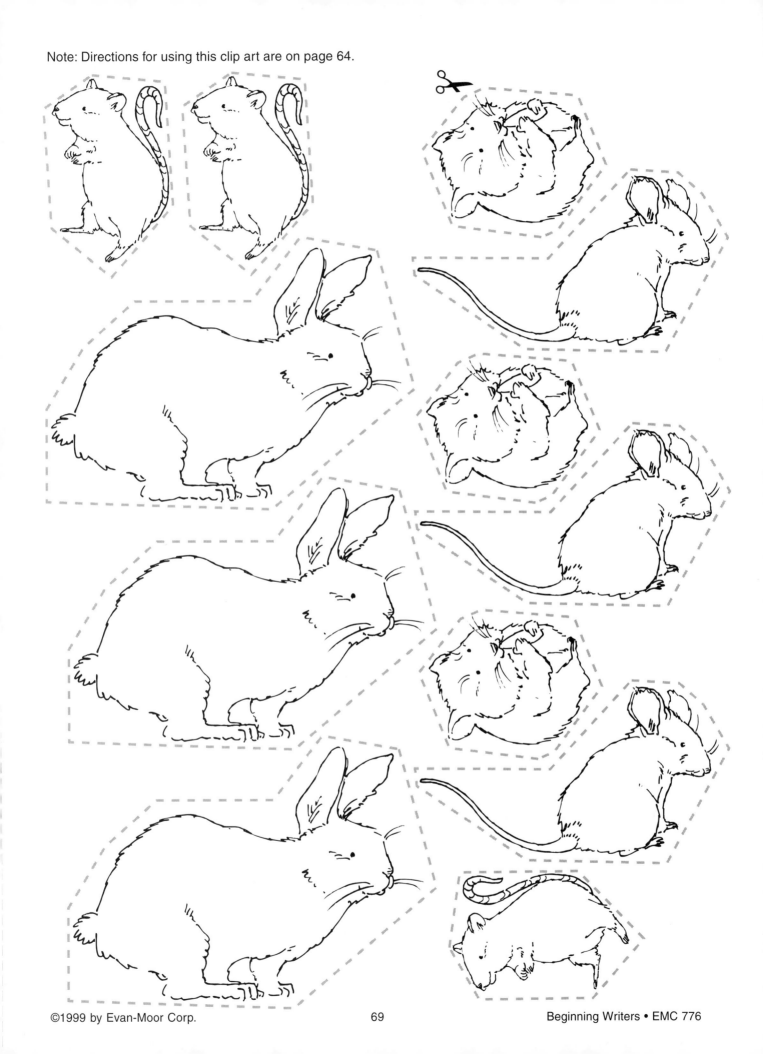

Chicken Coop

Prewriting Activities

Read

Emma's Eggs by Margariet Ruurs; Stoddart Kids, 1997.

Inside an Egg by Sylvia A. Johnson; Lerner Publications Company, 1987.

Kele's Secret by Tololwa M. Mollel; Lodestar Books, 1997.

The Chicken Sisters by Laura Joffe Numeroff; HarperCollins Juvenile Books, 1997.

Rosie's Walk by Pat Hutchins; Aladdin Paperbacks, 1973.

Hattie and the Fox by Mem Fox; Aladdin Paperbacks, 1992.

Chickens Aren't the Only Ones by Ruth Heller; Price Stern Sloan, 1993.

Get Ready to Write

1. Bring in a real chicken, toy chickens, or photographs of chickens. Ask students to describe the chicken and name its important parts (feathers, beak, tail, leg, etc.).

2. Discuss the names of the members of the chicken family. Ask students to tell something each of the chickens can do (*roosters crow, hens lay eggs, chickens scratch for food, chicks run after Mother Hen*). Have students make each chicken's sound.

   Extend the activity by playing "Follow the Chicken" on the playground. The leader acts out the walk and sound of a hen, rooster, or chick. The other students follow, copying the movement and sound.

Writing Activities

Individual Books

- **Draw a Story**
  Reproduce the cover and several blank pages.
  Help students think of their own topics for stories
  or use one of the following ideas:

  A Chicken Family
  Students draw a different bird in the coop on each
  page (rooster, hen, chick).

  Mrs. Hen and Her Chicks
  Students draw Mrs. Hen doing something with her
  chicks. Some students may want to dictate or write
  a phrase about what she is doing.

- **Complete the Sentences**
  Reproduce the cover, a blank form, and the cloze form.
  Students complete the sentences to create a story and
  then draw a picture on the blank form.

- **Write a Story**
  Reproduce the cover and several lined forms. Students
  write their own chicken stories. Possible story starters:

A Chicken Family	*The Naughty Little Chick*
In a Chicken Coop	*A Surprise in Mrs. Hen's Nest*
The Rooster That Lost His Crow	*Little Red Hen (retell the fairy tale)*

Group Books

- **Mother Hen's Chicks—A Chicken Counting Book**
  Reproduce a blank coop form and one or more copies
  of the clip art on page 76 for each student. Students will
  color, cut out, and paste the hen and an assigned number
  of chicks to the blank coop page. They will then write the
  number of chicks at the bottom of the page. This can be
  a simple phrase (*3 chicks*) or a complete sentence
  (*Mother Hen has 3 chicks.*). Place the pages in
  numerical order and attach a cover.

- **Chick Says "Cheep"—A Sound Book**
  Give students a blank coop form and a chick from
  page 76. Brainstorm /ch/ words. Have students paste
  the chick to the blank coop and draw a /ch/ object or action.
  They will then write or dictate a phrase about the picture.
  Compile student pages and attach a cover.

cover

cloze form

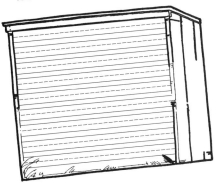

lined form for
written stories

clip art

Note: Reproduce this book cover for each student.

Beginning Writers • EMC 776

Note: Reproduce this page to draw a picture story or to use as a back cover.

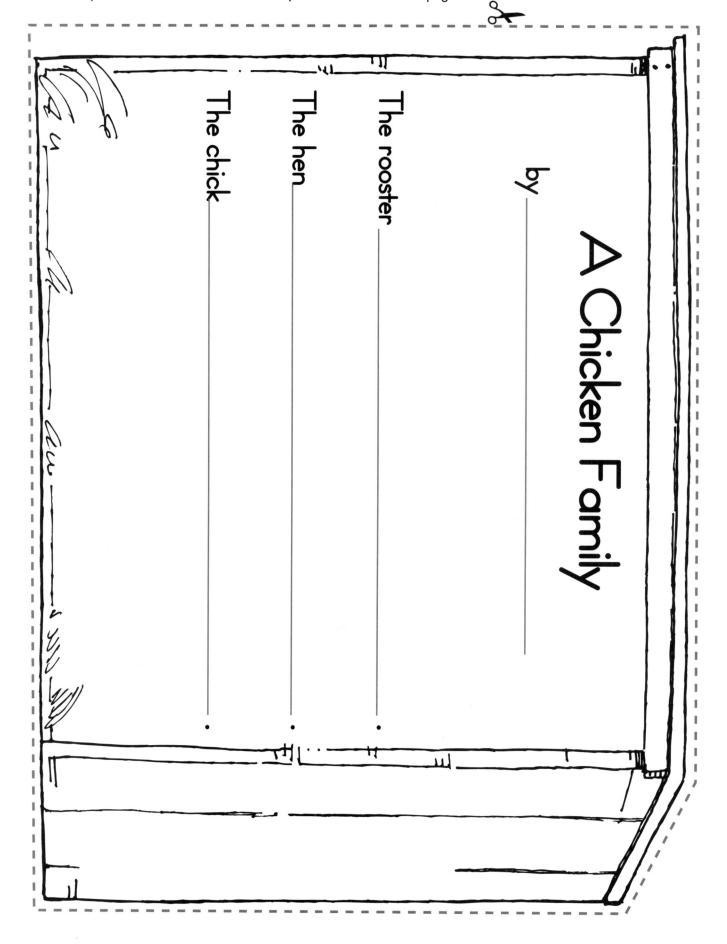

A Chicken Family

by _____

The rooster _____.

The hen _____.

The chick _____.

Note: Directions for using this clip art are on page 71.

Toolbox

Prewriting Activities

Read

Tool Book by Gail Gibbons; Holiday House, 1988.
Tools by Ann Morris; Mulberry Books, 1988.
Building a House by Byron Barton; Mulberry
  Books, 1990.
How a House Is Built by Gail Gibbons;
  Holiday House, 1996.
The House I'll Build for the Wrens by
  Shirley Neitzel; Greenwillow, 1997.

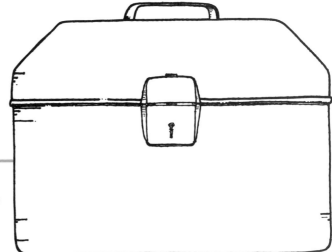

Get Ready to Write

1. Bring in a toolbox containing common
   tools (hammer, wrench, pliers, screwdriver,
   etc.) and other small hand tools (saw,
   plane, etc.). Work with students to name
   each tool and explain how it is used.
   Demonstrate how each tool is used.

2. Set up a tool center area where students
   can use tools. You will need to provide
   supervision as students hammer nails,
   saw wood, etc. Have students write about
   their experiences using tools.

Writing Activities

Individual Books

- **Draw a Story**
  Reproduce the cover and several blank pages.
  Help students think of their own topics for
  stories or use one of the following ideas:

  In _____'s Toolbox
  Have students draw a different tool on each
  page. Students may want to label the tools.

  We Go Together
  Students draw a tool and the item it is used
  with on each blank page (hammer and nail,
  screwdriver and screw, saw and wood).

- **Complete the Sentences**
  Reproduce the cover, a blank form, and the cloze form.
  Students complete the sentences to create a story and
  then draw a picture on the blank form.

- **Write a Story**
  Reproduce the cover and several lined forms. Students
  write their own toolbox stories. Possible story starters:

Mrs. Fix-It's Toolbox	*The Empty Toolbox*
Bang Bang, the Talking Hammer	*The First Hammer*
In My Toolbox	*Building a Doghouse*

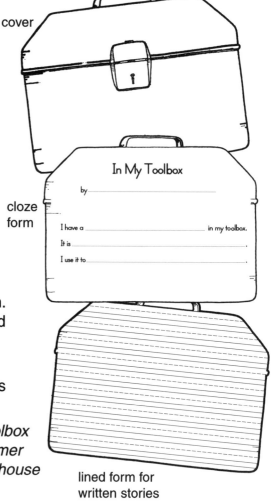

cover

cloze form

In My Toolbox

by _____

I have a _____ in my toolbox.

It is _____.

I use it to _____

lined form for
written stories

Group Books

- **Name the Tool—A Riddle Book**
  Each student will need a lined form. Model how to write
  a riddle about a tool. Include what the tool is made of,
  any sound it might make, and its function. Then have
  students select a tool and write a riddle on the form.
  On the back of the paper, draw the tool or paste a
  picture from the clip art on page 83. Compile student
  pages with the riddle face up and attach a cover.

- **The Magic Toolbox**
  Students will need one or more lined forms. Discuss
  the ways in which a tool might be "magic" (can talk,
  work by itself, fly, etc.). Have students select a
  tool and write a story about a magical
  experience. Compile student pages
  and attach a cover.

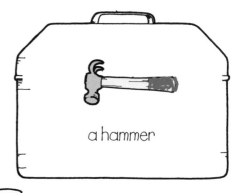

a hammer

clip art

Note: Reproduce this book cover for each student.

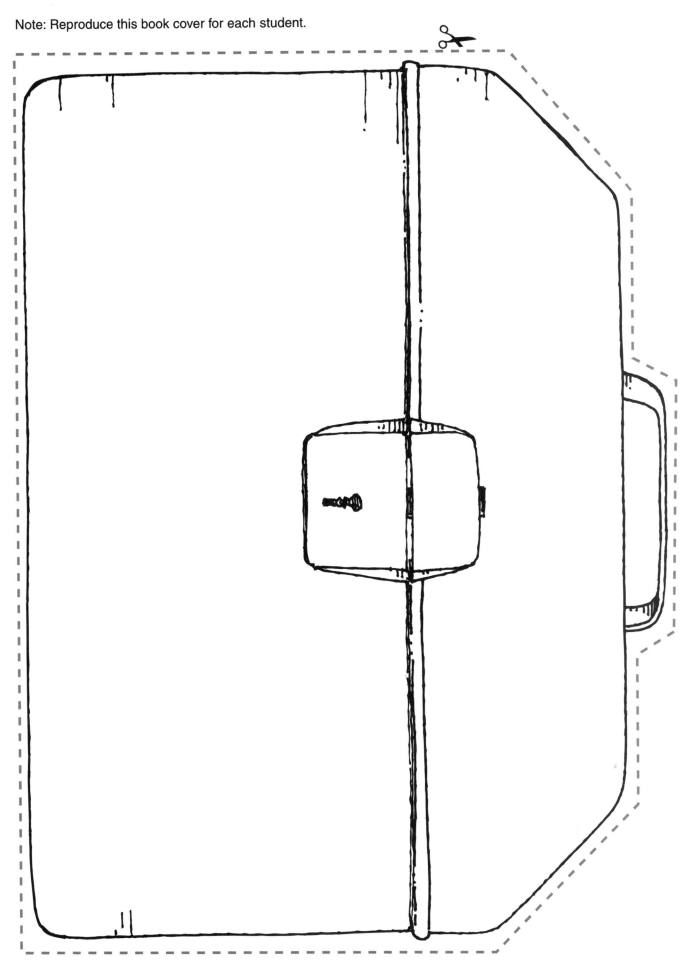

 Beginning Writers • EMC 776

Note: Reproduce this page to draw a picture story or to use as a back cover.

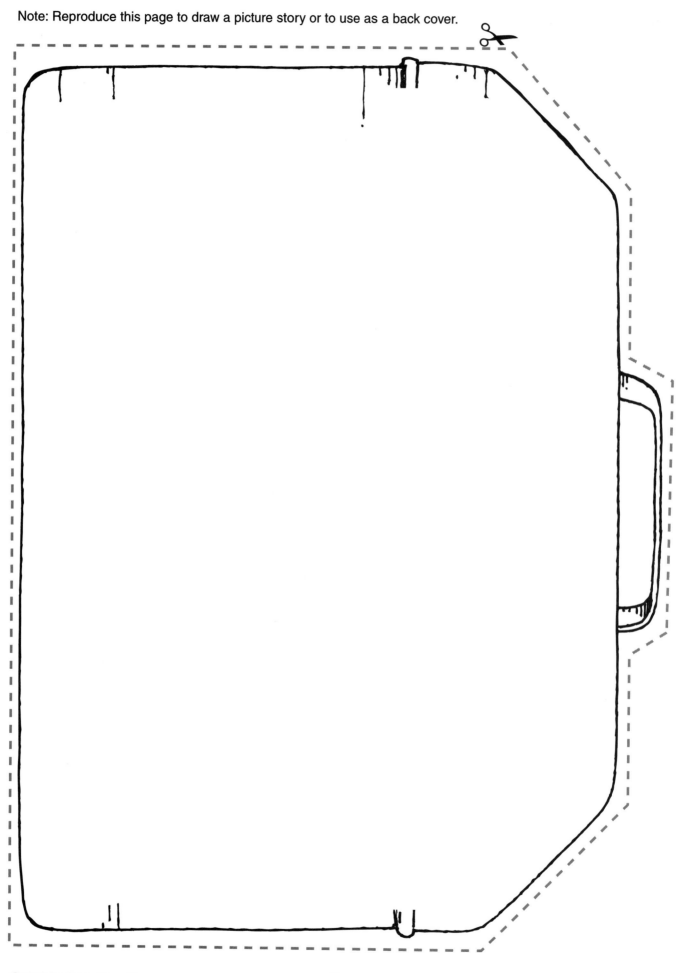

Beginning Writers • EMC 776

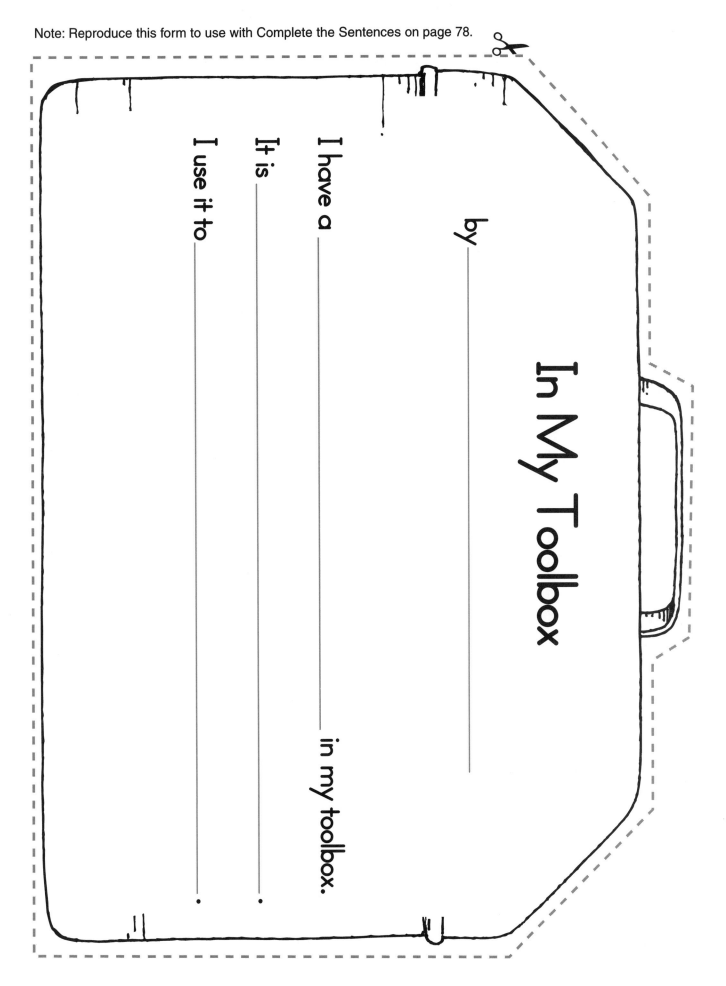

In My Toolbox

by _____

I have a _____ in my toolbox.

It is _____.

I use it to _____.

Note: Reproduce this page for written stories.

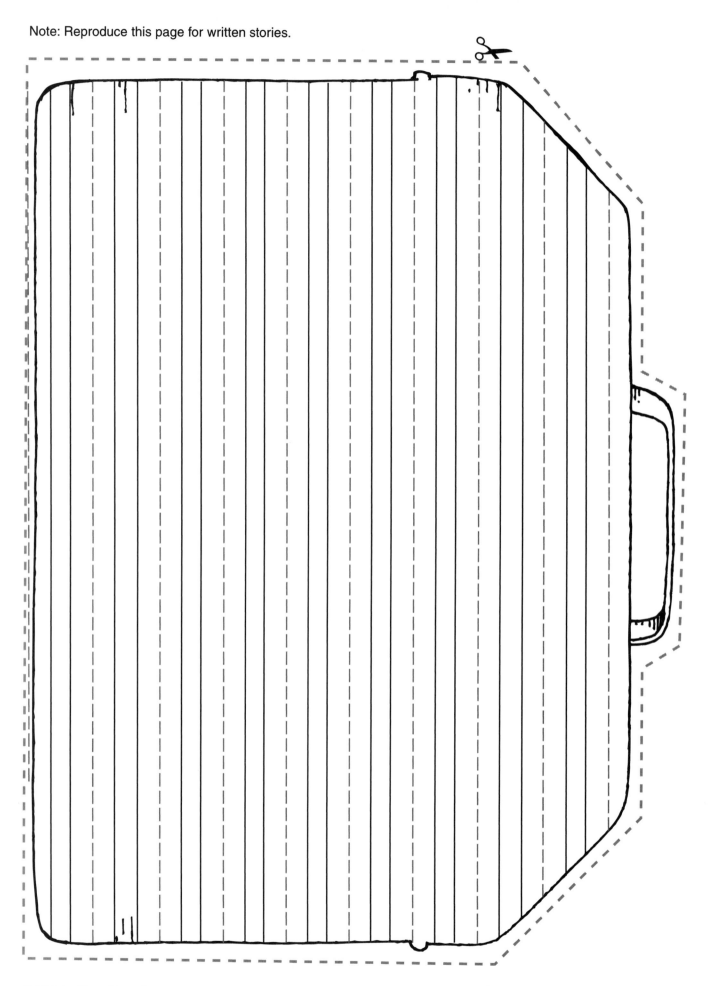

Beginning Writers • EMC 776

Note: Directions for using this clip art are on page 78.

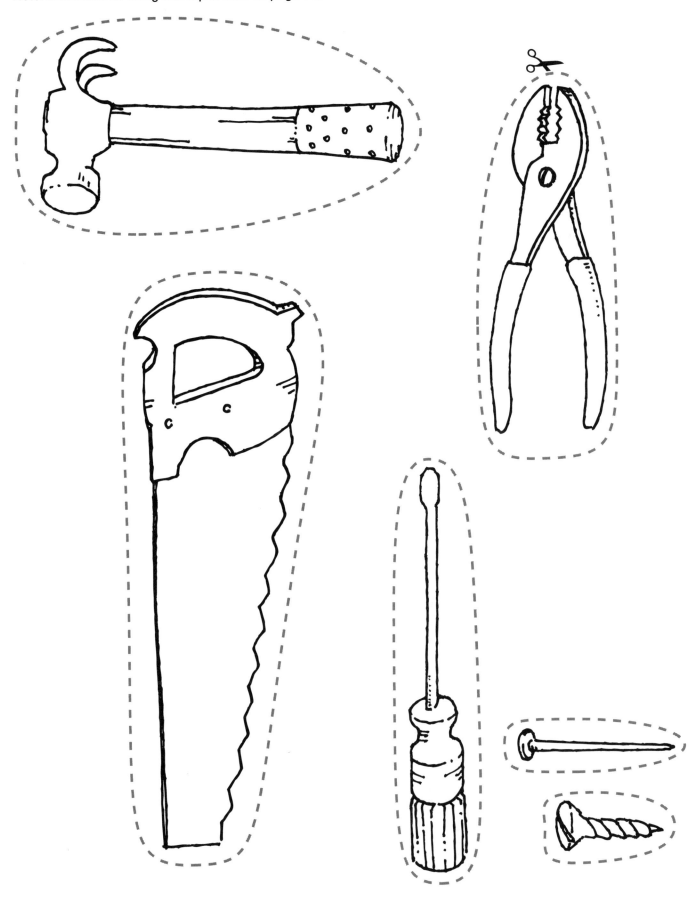

Beginning Writers • EMC 776

Prewriting Activities

Read

The Dream Jar by Bonnie Pryor; William
Morrow & Company Library, 1996.
Stop That Pickle! by Peter Armour; Houghton
Mifflin Company, 1993.
The Lemon Drop Jar by Christine Widman;
Simon & Schuster, 1992.
The Mysterious Tadpole by Steven Kellogg;
Demco Media, 1977.
*Pets in a Jar: Collecting and Caring for
Small Wild Animals* by Seymour Simon;
Viking Press, 1988.

Get Ready to Write

1. Bring in one or more full jars (pickles,
   peanut butter, jam, etc.). Cover the jars
   with construction paper so students
   cannot see the contents. Ask students
   to guess what is in the jar(s). At first have
   them guess based on what they know
   comes in jars. Then give hints to help
   them reach the correct answer. Take time
   to sample the contents.

2. Have students give examples of ways their
   families use empty jars (recycle glass, store
   leftovers, save nails, buttons, etc.). Discuss
   things that they might keep in empty jars
   (pennies, marbles, broken crayons,
   fishing worms, etc.).

Writing Activities

Individual Books

- **Draw a Story**
  Reproduce the cover and several blank pages.
  Help students think of their own topics for stories
  or use one of the following ideas:

  A Jar of _____
  On each page, students are to draw and label
  a different item they might save in a jar
  (buttons, shells, tadpoles, etc.).

  Paint Jars—A Book of Colors
  Students paint each jar a different color.
  They write the color of the paint across
  the jar using black paint and a thin brush.
  After the paint has dried, have students
  cut out the jars and add a cover.

- **Complete the Sentences**
  Reproduce the cover, a blank form, and the cloze form.
  Students complete the sentences to create a story and
  then draw a picture on the blank form.

- **Write a Story**
  Reproduce the cover and several lined forms. Students
  write their own jar stories. Possible story starters:

Jam Jar	*How to Make an Ant Farm in a Jar*
Catching _____	*Grandma's Button Jar*
What Is In the Jar?	*How to Keep Worms in a Jar*

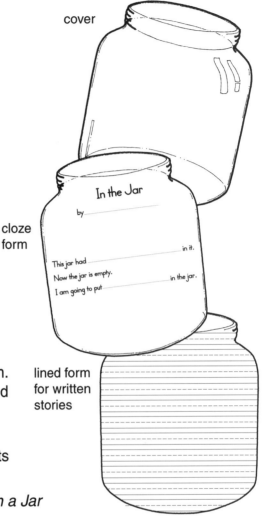

cover

cloze form

In the Jar
by _____

This jar had _____ in it.
Now the jar is empty.
I am going to put _____ in the jar.

lined form
for written
stories

Group Books

- **How Many Jelly Beans?**
  Give each student a blank jar form and a supply of jelly beans
  from page 90. Students color five or less jelly beans red and
  five or less jelly beans green. They then cut out the jelly beans
  and paste them on the jar. Have students write a math sentence
  about the jelly beans (3 red + 4 green = 7 jelly beans) at the
  bottom of the jar. Compile student pages and attach a cover.

- **Tasty Treats**
  Each student needs a blank jar form and a lined form. Brainstorm
  and list things to eat that come in a jar. Have students draw a
  tasty treat inside the jar. On the lined form, they are to write
  a description of the treat including how it looks, smells, and tastes.
  Compile student pages and attach a cover.

4 + 2 = 6

clip art

Beginning Writers • EMC 776

Note: Reproduce this book cover for each student.

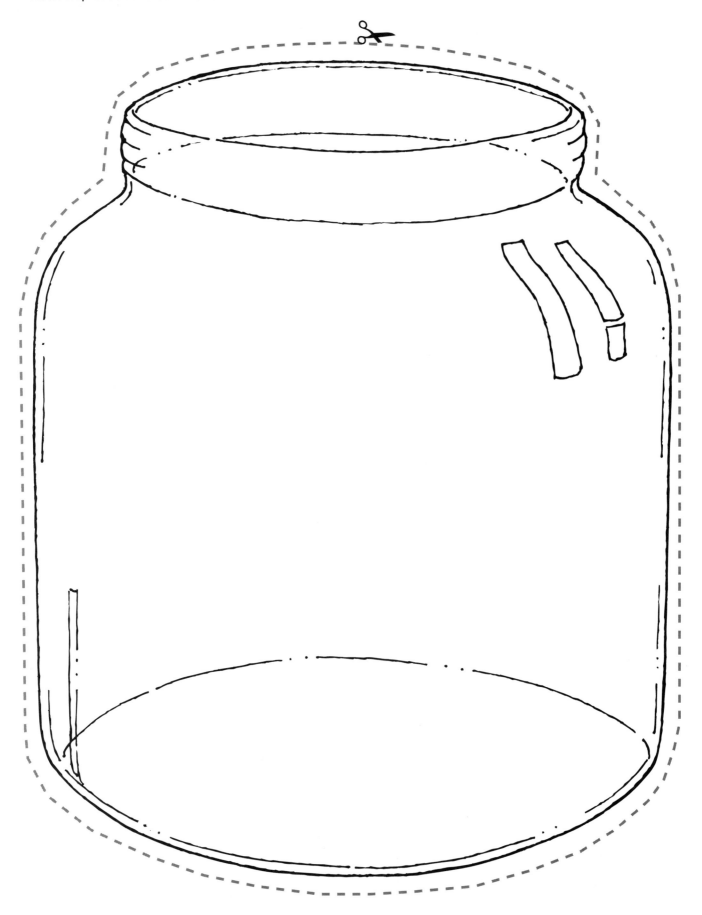

Note: Reproduce this page to draw a picture story or to use as a back cover.

 Beginning Writers • EMC 776

In the Jar

by _____

This jar had _____ in it.

Now the jar is empty.

I am going to put _____ in the jar.

Beginning Writers • EMC 776

Note: Reproduce this page for written stories.

Note: Directions for using this clip art are on page 85.

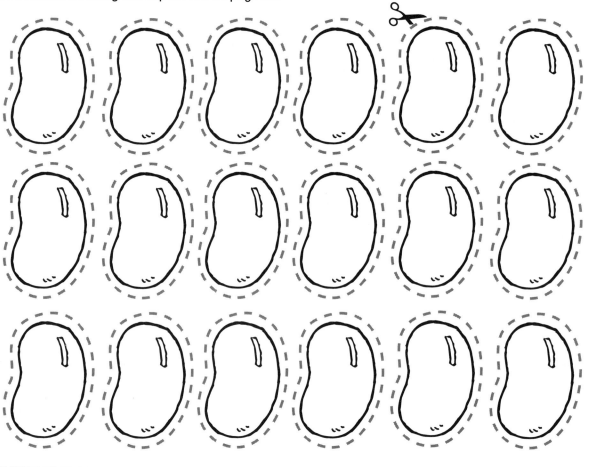

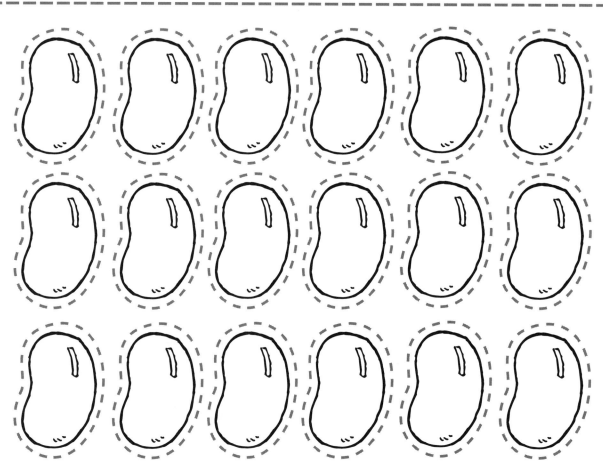

90

Shoes

Prewriting Activities

Read

Alligator Shoes by Arthur Dorros; E. P. Dutton, 1992.

Shoes Like Miss Alice's by Angela Johnson; Orchard Books, 1995.

Flip-Flops by Nancy Cole; Albert Whitman & Company, 1998.

A Pair of Red Sneakers by Lisa Lawston; Orchard Books, 1998.

Benjamin Bigfoot by Mary Serfozo; Margaret McElderry, 1993.

Sam's Sneaker Search by Claire O'Brien; Simon & Schuster, 1997.

The Bootmaker and the Elves by Susan Lowell; Orchard Books, 1997.

Get Ready to Write

1. Brainstorm and list kinds of shoes. Have students examine the various types of shoes classmates have worn to school. Then have students sort themselves into groups by the different types of shoes (sneakers, sandals, boots, etc.), by color of shoes (brown, black, red, etc.), or by types of closures (lace-up, Velcro® snaps, no closures, etc.). Extend the lesson by graphing the number of students wearing each type of shoe.

2. Bring in shoes for various uses. Include rain boots, cowboy boots, bedroom slippers, tap shoes, sports shoes with cleats, ballet slippers, pumps, etc. Discuss the shoe names and functions.

Writing Activities

Individual Books

- **Draw a Story**
  Reproduce the cover and several blank pages. Help students think of their own topics for stories or use one of the following ideas:

  My Favorite Shoes
  On each blank form, students will draw a different type of shoe they like.

  Old Shoes, New Shoes
  On each blank form, students are to draw one old shoe and one new shoe.

- **Complete the Sentences**
  Reproduce the cover, a blank form, and the cloze form. Students complete the sentences to create a story and then draw a picture on the blank form.

- **Write a Story**
  Reproduce the cover and several lined forms. Students write their own shoe stories. Possible story starters:

At the Shoe Store	*One Lost Shoe*
Wearing Mom's (Dad's) Shoes	*Old Sneakers*
(storybook character)'s Shoes	*Dancing Feet*

Group Books

- **Who Wears This Shoe?**
  Students will need a copy of the lined shoe box form. Reproduce a number of copies of the clip art on page 97 and cut the shoes apart. Allow students to choose a shoe. They are to color and cut out the shoe, and glue it to the back of the writing page. Students then write a riddle about the shoe including what it is made of, what it is used for, and a hint about who wears it. Model the activity before students begin. (*This shoe is make of rubber. It keeps feet dry. It is worn by someone who puts out fires. Answer–fire fighter's boot.*) Compile student pages and attach a cover.

- **A Trip to the Shoe Store**
  Reproduce one or more lined forms for each student. They are to write about a trip to the shoe store to buy new shoes. Encourage students to describe the shoes and tell where they will wear them. Students may draw the shoes or paste on a shoe from page 97.

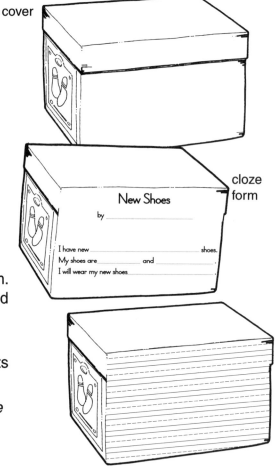

cover

cloze form

lined form for written stories

Note: Reproduce this book cover for each student.

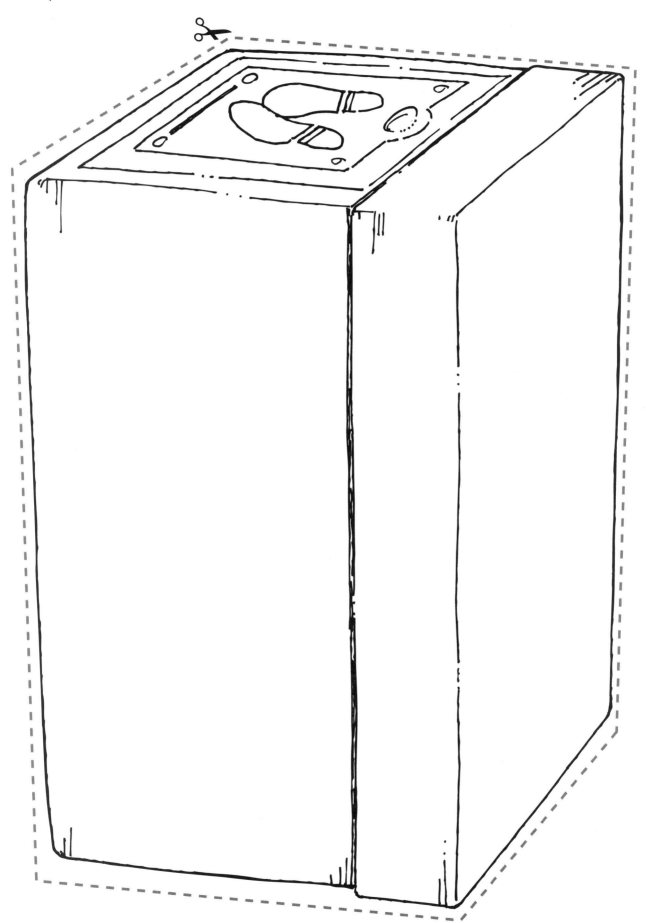

 Beginning Writers • EMC 776

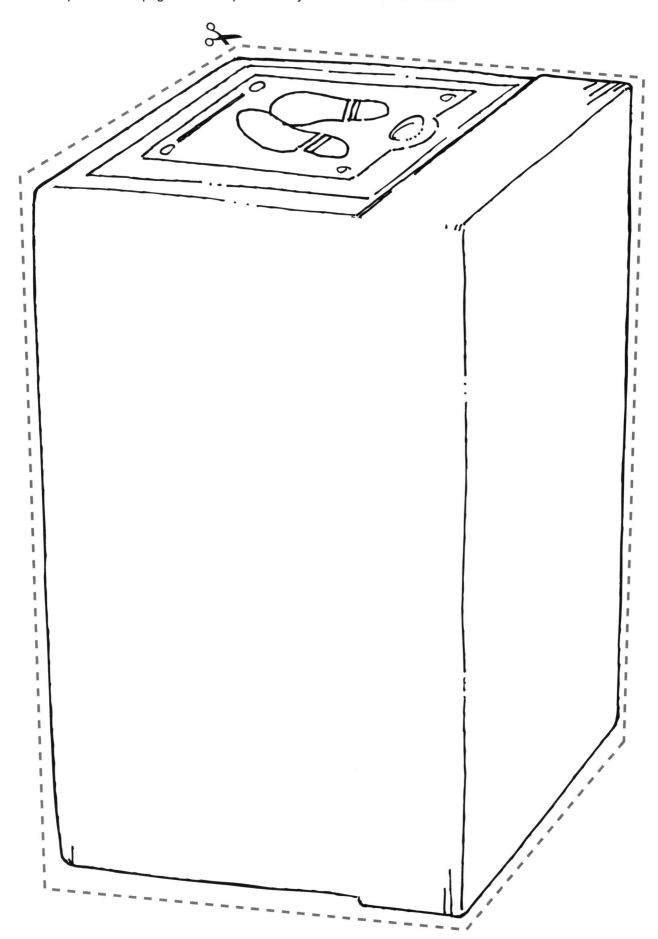

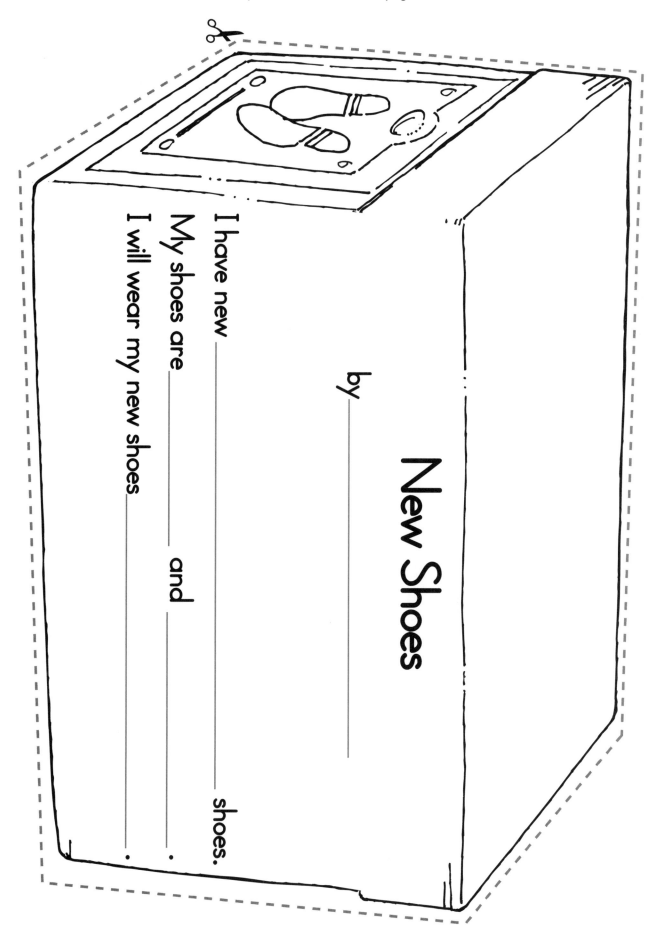

I have new _____ shoes.

My shoes are _____ and _____.

I will wear my new shoes _____.

New Shoes

by _____

Note: Reproduce this page for written stories.

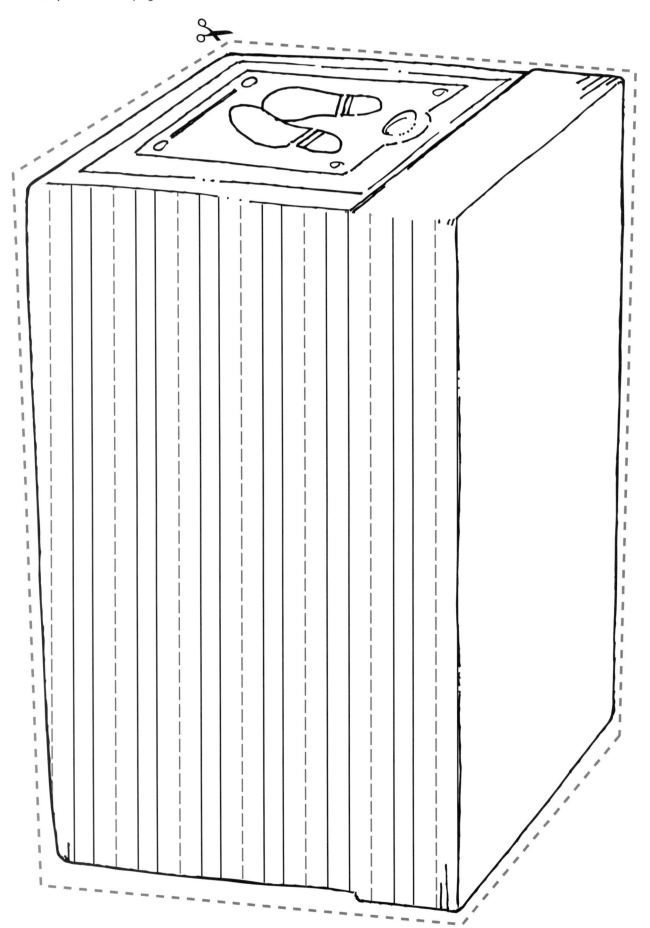

Note: Directions for using this clip art are on page 92.

Beginning Writers • EMC 776

Prewriting Activities

Read

Pen Pals by Joan Holub; Grosset & Dunlap, 1997.
The Long Long Letter by Elizabeth Spurr;
  Hyperion Press, 1996.
A Letter to Amy by Ezra Jack Keats;
  Puffin, 1998.
Stringbean's Trip to the Shining Sea by
  Vera B. Williams; William Morrow &
  Company Library, 1988.
*The Jolly Postman: Or Other People's
  Letters* by Janet Ahlberg and Allan
  Ahlberg; Little, Brown & Company, 1986.
Dear Mr. Blueberry by Simon James;
  Margaret McElderry, 1991.

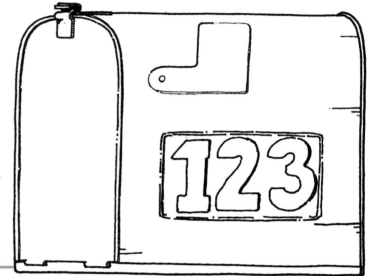

Get Ready to Write

1. Decorate a box to resemble a mailbox.
   Fill it with examples of things that come
   through the mail (letter, invitation, greeting
   card, thank-you note, post card, bill, small
   gift, magazine, advertisements). Brainstorm
   and list kinds of things that can be found in a
   mailbox. As students name items, pull an
   example from the "mailbox." Share any types
   of items not named by students.

2. Invite a mail carrier to speak to the class about
   his or her job. As a follow-up, let students take
   turns delivering class mail. Prepare an envelope
   addressed to each student. Place the envelopes
   in a bag to represent the mail carrier's pouch.
   Each student gets a turn to take an envelope
   from the pouch and deliver it to the
   correct person in class.

Writing Activities

Individual Books

• **Draw a Story**
Reproduce the cover and several blank pages.
Help students think of their own topics for stories
or use one of the following ideas:

I Found It in My Mailbox
On each page students will draw a different item
that could be found in a mailbox.

There's a Package in the Mail
Remind students that packages sometimes
come in the mail. On one blank form,
they are to draw themselves getting a
package out of the mailbox and then draw
what was in the package on another form.

• **Complete the Sentences**
Reproduce the cover, a blank form, and the cloze form.
Students complete the sentences to create a story and
then draw a picture on the blank form.

• **Write a Story**
Reproduce the cover and several lined forms. Students
write their own mailbox stories. Possible story starters:

Come to My Party	*A Funny Message*
The Magic Mail Box	*Maggie (Martin), the Mail Carrier*
A Letter to _____	*A Letter from* _____

cover

cloze form

lined form for written stories

Group Books

• **Postcard to a Pen Pal**
Give students a copy of the postcard on page 104. Discuss what
a pen pal is. Have students decide who they would like for a pen
pal (real or make-believe). On the front of the postcard, they are
to draw a picture or write a message and then address the card.
Compile the postcards and attach a cover.

• **Happy Holidays**
Reproduce several copies of the clip art on page 104. Each student
will need a lined form, a stamp from page 104, and a real envelope. You will need one metal
ring to hold the completed project. Brainstorm and list the names of holidays. Students
decorate the edges of the lined form with a symbol representing a holiday and then write
a holiday message. Place the message in the envelope, making sure to fold it so that the
message will not be caught in the metal ring. Do not seal the envelope. Have students
address the envelope and glue a stamp in the corner. Compile student envelopes, punch
a hole in the upper left hand corner, and attach the envelopes with the metal ring.

Note: Reproduce this book cover for each student.

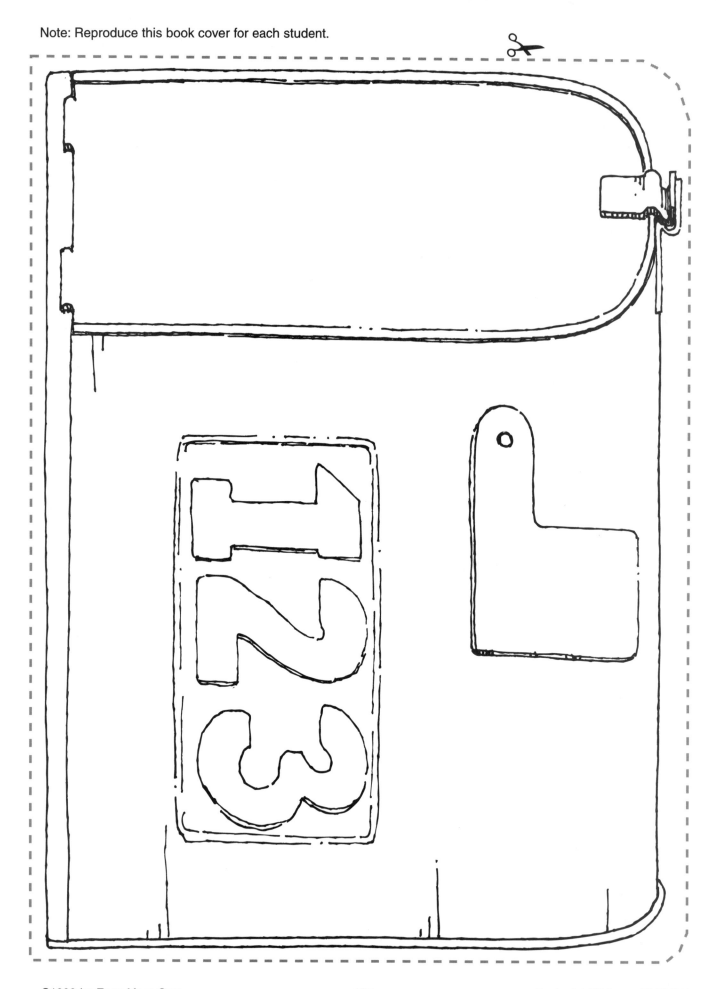

Beginning Writers • EMC 776

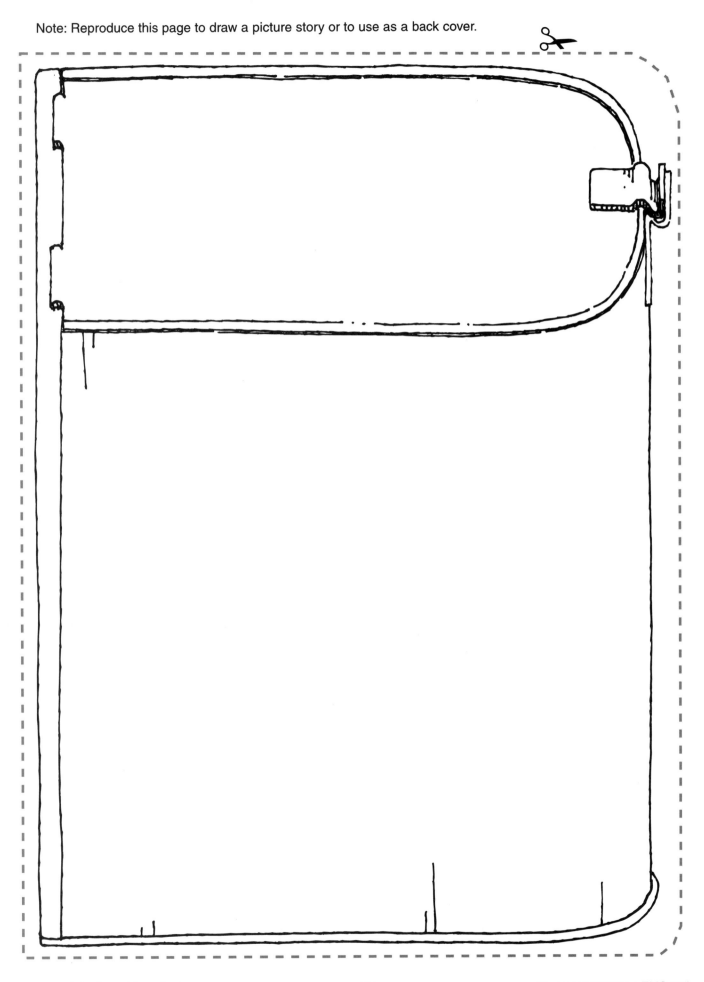

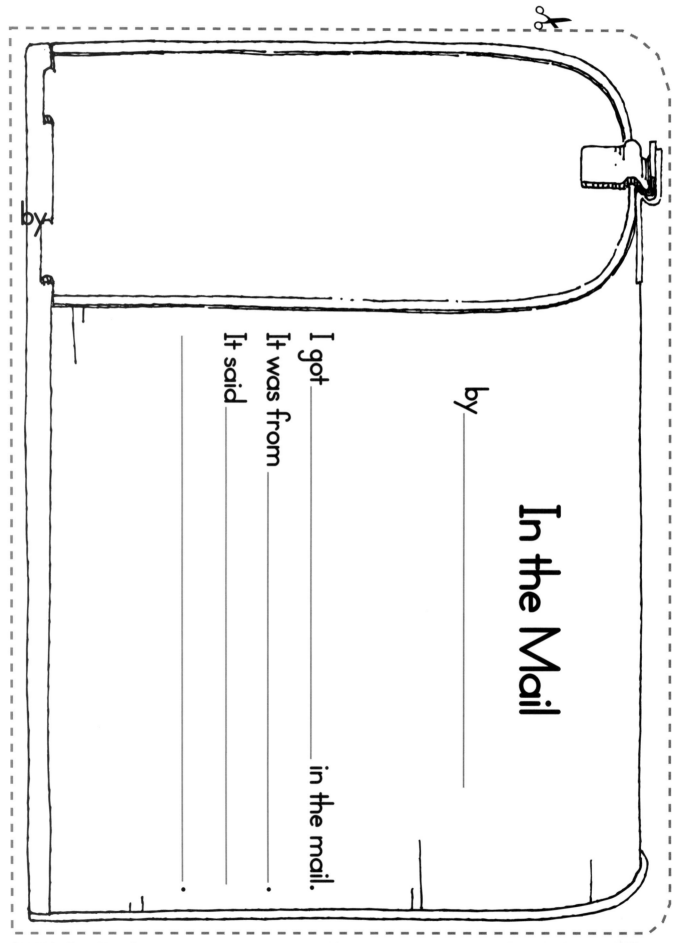

In the Mail

by _____

I got _____

It was from _____ in the mail.

It said _____ .

_____ .

by

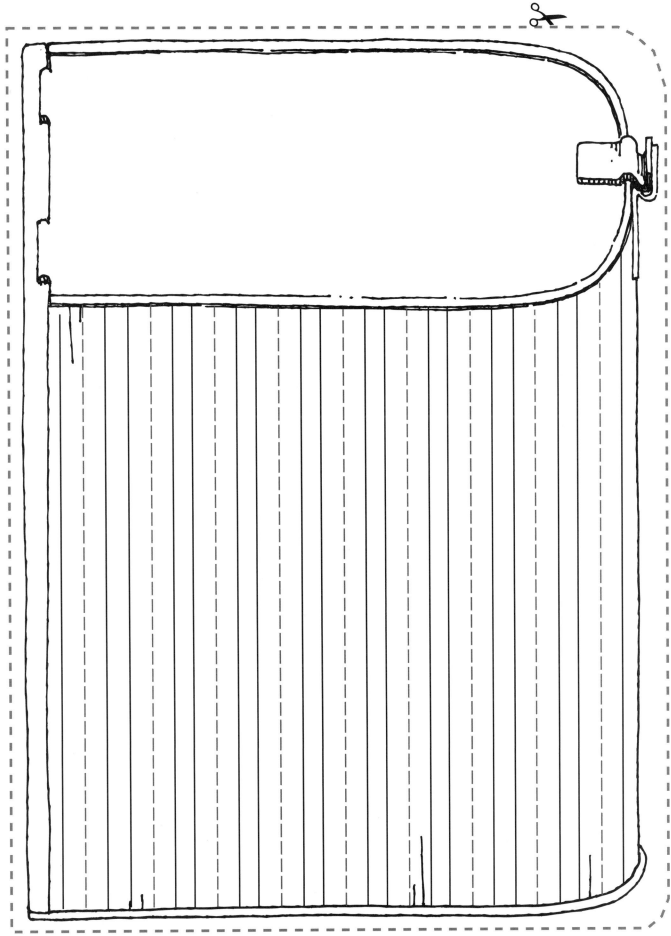

Beginning Writers • EMC 776

Note: Directions for using this clip art are on page 99.

Beginning Writers • EMC 776

Soup Pot

Prewriting Activities

Read

Alphabet Soup by Katherine Anne Banks; Knopf, 1994.
Boy Soup: Or When Giant Caught Cold by
  Loris Lesynski; Annick Press, 1996.
Button Soup by Doris Orgel; Bantam
  Doubleday Dell Publications, 1994.
*Watch Out for the Chicken Feet in
  Your Soup* by Tomie de Paola; Little
  Simon Books, 1985.
Stone Soup by Heather Forest; August
  House Little Folk, 1998.
Mean Soup by Betsy Everitt;
  Harcourt Brace, 1995.
Monster Stew by Mitra Modarressi;
  DK Inc., 1998.

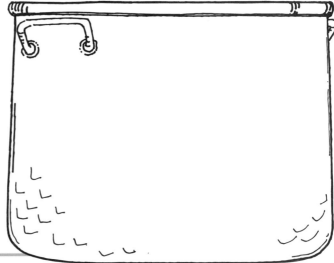

Get Ready to Write

1. Brainstorm kinds of soup. Ask students to name
   what they think is in each kind of soup. Have an
   assortment of canned soups on hand. Read the
   main ingredients on the can. Have students name
   their favorite kind of soup. Graph the results.

2. Share a version of *Stone Soup* with your students.
   Ask each student to name one item to put in the
   stone soup. List the items to create a "recipe" for soup.

   Follow up the activity by making stone soup in class.
   Bring in a clean stone, a large pot, and a heat source.
   Ask each student to bring one item for the soup.
   (Invite a few parents to aid in cleaning, cutting, and
   serving.) Cook the soup and enjoy
   eating it before writing
   soup stories.

Writing Activities

Individual Books

- **Draw a Story**
  Reproduce the cover and several blank pages.
  Help students think of their own topics for stories
  or use one of the following ideas:

  I Like Soup
  Students draw a can or bowl of their favorite
  kind of soup on one form and show themselves
  eating the soup on a second form.

  What's In the Soup Pot?
  Students draw a different soup ingredient
  on each page.

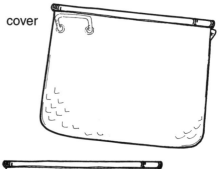

cover

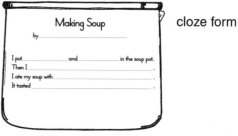

cloze form

- **Complete the Sentences**
  Reproduce the cover, a blank form, and the cloze form.
  Students complete the sentences to create a story and
  then draw a picture on the blank form.

- **Write a Story**
  Reproduce the cover and several lined forms. Students
  write their own soup stories. Possible story starters:

  Look Out for _____ in Your Soup!   *Spilled Soup*
  How to Make a Pot of Soup   *Yucky Soup*
  (story character)'s Favorite Soup   *Alligator Soup*

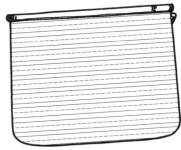

lined form for
written stories

Group Books

- **Making _____ Soup**
  Students will need a blank pot form and a lined form.
  They are to give their soup a name (it can realistic,
  e.g., vegetable soup, or unusual, e.g., purple soup).
  They then draw items (or paste pictures from page 111)
  in the pot and write a recipe for the soup on the lined
  form. Compile student "recipes" and attach the soup
  pot cover.

- **Alphabet Soup**
  Each student will need a blank soup pot form. Assign
  each student a letter of the alphabet. They are to draw
  an item beginning with their assigned letter and write
  a phrase about it at the bottom of the page (*a* is for
  alligator soup, *b* is for banana soup, *c* is for carrot
  soup, etc.). Compile student pages in alphabetical
  order and attach the soup pot cover.

clip art

Note: Reproduce this book cover for each student.

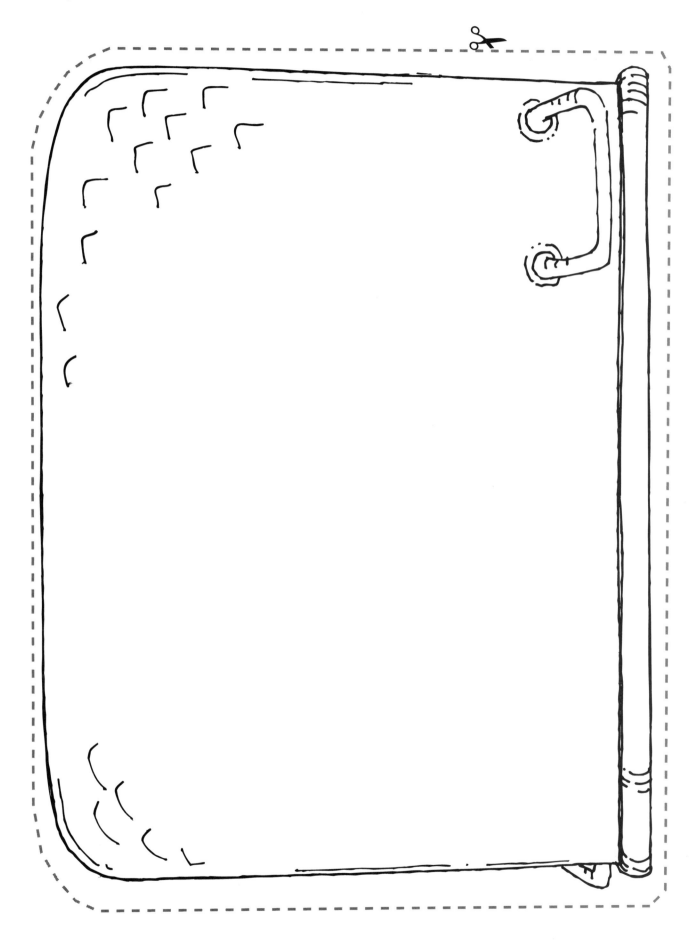

Note: Reproduce this page to draw a picture story or to use as a back cover.

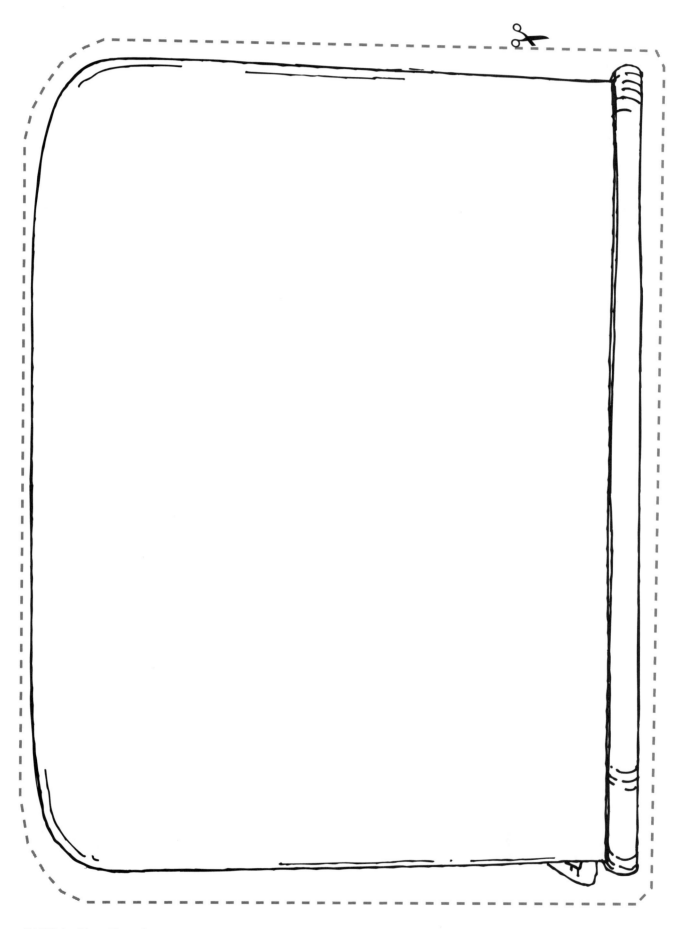

Beginning Writers • EMC 776

Note: Reproduce this form to use with Complete the Sentences on page 106.

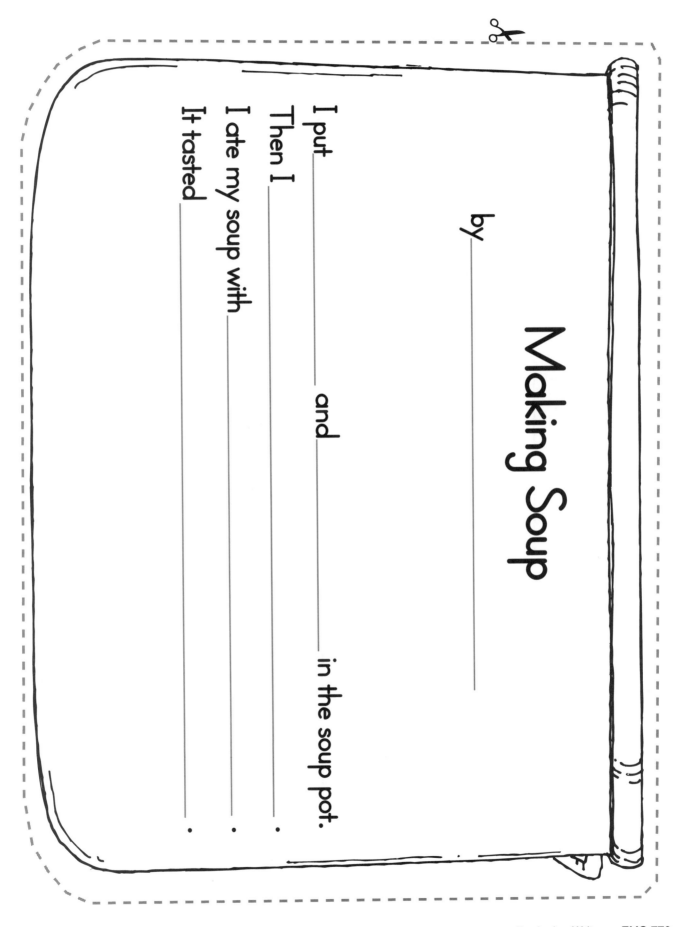

Making Soup

by _____

I put _____ and _____ in the soup pot.

Then I _____ .

I ate my soup with _____ .

It tasted _____ .

Beginning Writers • EMC 776

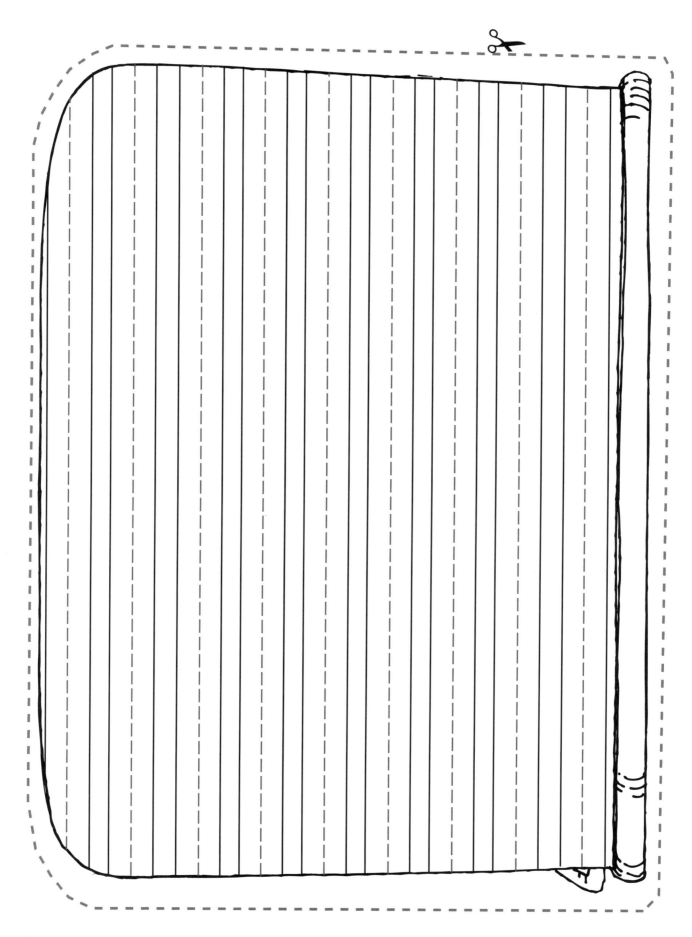

Note: Directions for using this clip art are on page 106.

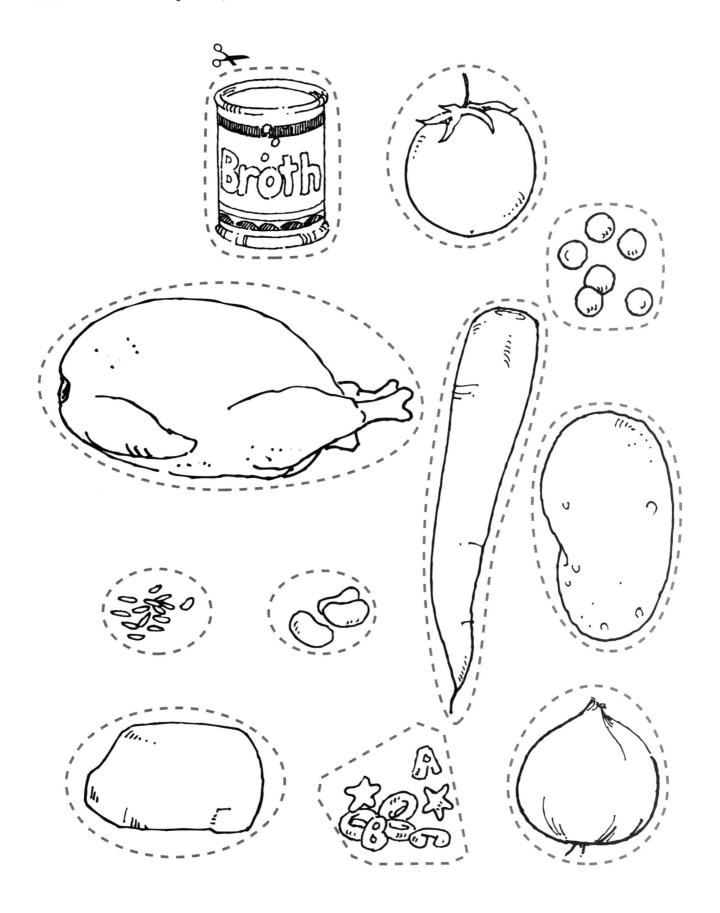

 # Seed Packet

Prewriting Activities

Read

The Butterfly Seeds by Mary Watson; William Morrow, 1995.

From Seed to Plant by Gail Gibbons; Holiday House, 1993.

Dandelion Adventures by L. Patricia Kite; Millbrook Press Trade, 1998.

Jack and the Beanstalk by Paul Galdone; Houghton Mifflin Company, 1982.

The Carrot Seed by Ruth Krauss; HarperCollins Juvenile Books, 1988.

The Surprise Garden by Zoe Hall; Scholastic Trade, 1998.

Anno's Magic Seeds by Mitsumasa Anno; Philomel Books, 1995.

Get Ready to Write

1. Bring in an assortment of seed packets to share with students. Explore the pictures and information on the packets. Open them and examine the seeds. Compare sizes, shapes, and colors of the various kinds of seeds. Discuss where seeds come from. (You may want to have several pieces of fruit on hand to show where some seeds develop.) Ask students to explain what happens when seeds are planted.

2. Plant seeds from one or more seed packets in pots in the classroom. Select fast-growing items such as beans, radishes, or nasturtiums. Have students share in the care of the plants and in recording observations of the growth.

 Beginning Writers • EMC 776

Writing Activities

Individual Books

• **Draw a Story**

Reproduce the cover and several blank pages. Help students think of their own topics for stories or use one of the following ideas:

Seeds
Students will draw a seed picture (or paste a seed picture from page 118) on each blank form. Have students write or dictate the name of the plant under the seed.

Growing Seeds
Each student will draw three pages showing the growth of a seed—a seed being planted, a sprouting plant, and a mature plant. Assemble the pages in order.

• **Complete the Sentences**

Reproduce the cover, a blank form, and the cloze form. Students complete the sentences to create a story and then draw a picture on the blank form.

• **Write a Story**

Reproduce the cover and several lined forms. Students write their own seed and plant stories. Possible story starters:

A Seed Grows   *Weeds in My Garden*
Little Mouse's Garden   *Who Ate the Sunflower Seeds?*
Magic _____ Seeds   *What to Do with a Seed*

cover

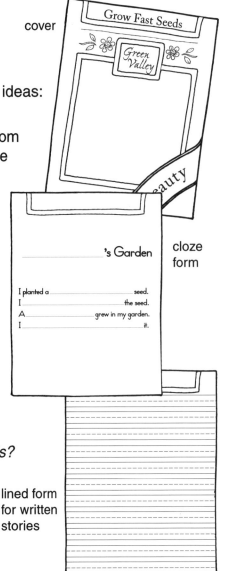

cloze form

lined form for written stories

Group Books

• **Seed Catalog**

Reproduce the seed packet cover and a lined form for each student. They are to draw a plant picture (or paste a picture from page 118) in the center of the seed packet. They then write directions for growing the seed on the lined form and paste their directions to the back of the seed packet form. Compile student "seed catalog" pages and attach a cover, binding the book at the top.

• **The Magic Seeds**

Students will use lined forms to write variations of *Jack and the Beanstalk*. After discussing the original story, explain to students that they can write about real plant seeds that happen to grow in an unusual way or imaginary seeds (car seeds, bubble-gum seeds, etc.) that grow into unusual plants. Have students illustrate their stories. Compile the stories and attach a cover.

Note: Reproduce this book cover for each student.

Grow Fast Seeds

Green Valley

Beauty

Beginning Writers • EMC 776

Note: Reproduce this page to draw a picture story or to use as a back cover.

115

Note: Reproduce this form to use with Complete the Sentences on page 113.

_____'s Garden

I planted a _____ seed.

I _____the seed.

A _____ grew in my garden.

I _____it.

 Beginning Writers • EMC 776

Note: Reproduce this page for written stories.

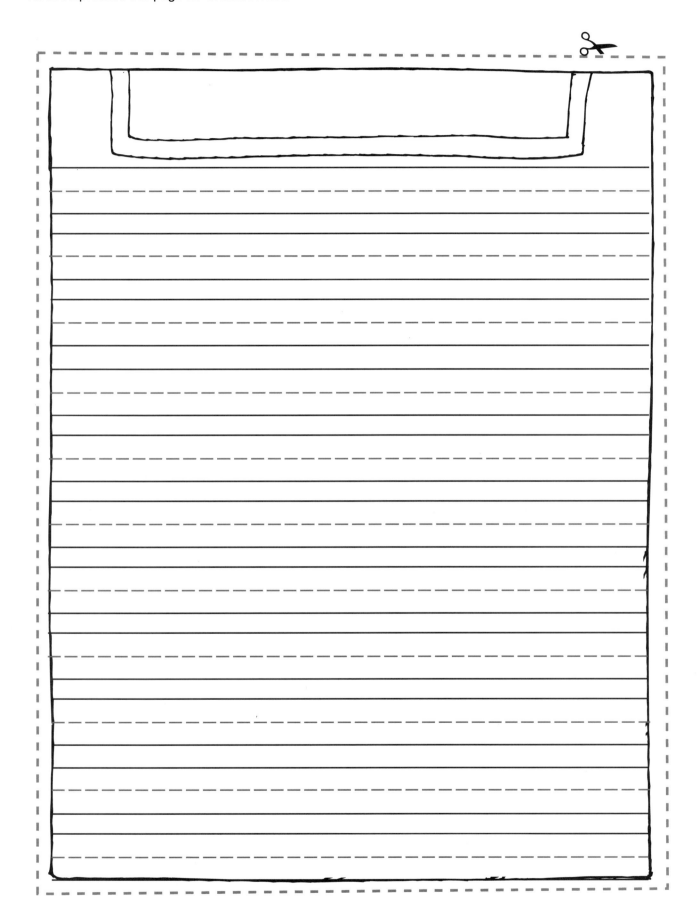

Note: Directions for using this clip art are on page 113.

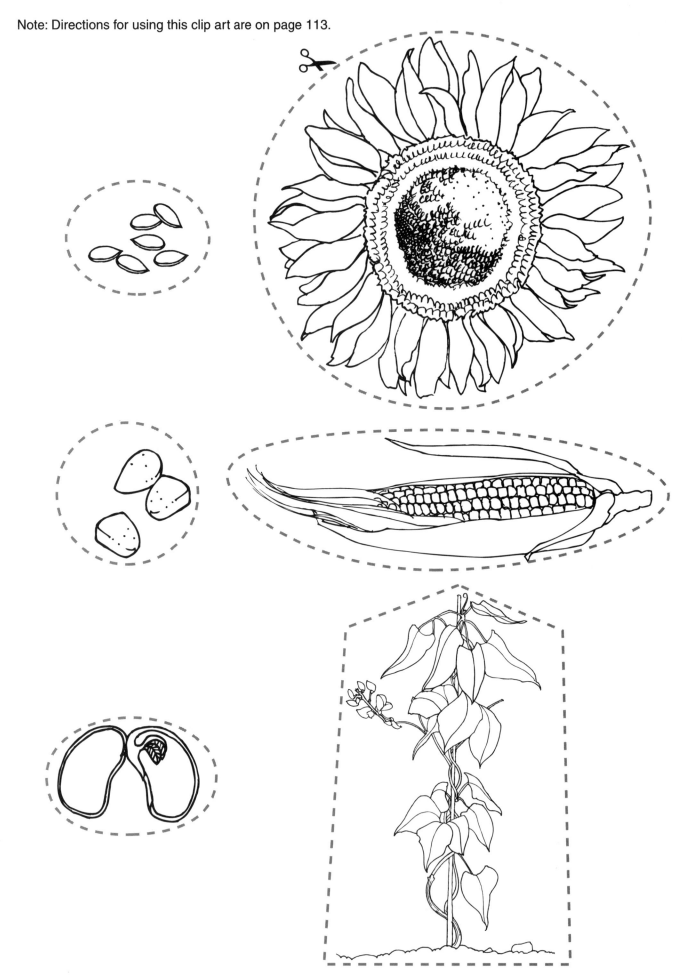

Purse

Prewriting Activities

Read

The Big Green Pocketbook by Candice F. Ransom;
  Harper Trophy, 1995.
Lilly's Purple Plastic Purse by Kevin Henkes;
  Greenwillow, 1996.
The Lady with the Alligator Purse by
  Nadine Bernard Westcott; Little, Brown
  & Company, 1990.
The Purse by Kathy Caple; Sandpiper, 1992.
Riddle of the Red Purse by Patricia Reilly
  and Blanche Sims; Young Yearling, 1987.

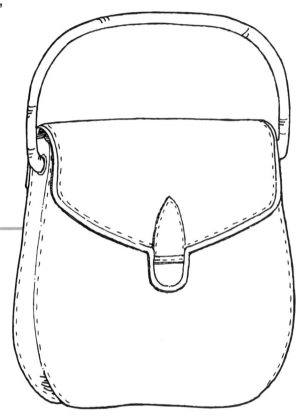

Get Ready to Write

1. Bring in a purse containing "typical" items.
    Ask students to think of items that might be
    carried in the purse. Open the purse to see
    if anything they named is in it. Ask students
    to think of things that would never be carried
    in a purse.

2. Name a character or real-life person known
    to the students (Cinderella, the school
    principal, Miss Frizzle, Fairy Godmother,
    Mrs. Bear of the Three Bears, etc.). Ask,
    "What would (character or person) carry
    in her purse?"

    Or play "Whose Purse Is It?" Describe
    an object that might be in the purse
    of a character or real-life person.
    (*This purse has a dust rag and a glass
    slipper. This purse contains a whistle,
    a red pen, and some happy-face stamps.*)

Writing Activities

Individual Books

- **Draw a Story**
  Reproduce the cover and several blank pages. Help students think of their own topics for stories or use one of the following ideas:

  In My Mom's Purse.
  On each blank page, students draw a different item they would find in their mother's purse.

  Gone Shopping
  Brainstorm places students might shop (bakery, grocery store, pet shop, toy store, bookstore, etc.) and what they would buy in the various stores. Give each student three blank pages on which to draw a thing "bought" at each of three different stores.

- **Complete the Sentences**
  Reproduce the cover, a blank form, and the cloze form. Students complete the sentences to create a story and then draw a picture on the blank form.

- **Write a Story**
  Reproduce the cover and several lined forms. Students write their own purse stories. Possible story starters:

Grandma's Purse	*My Mom's Purse is Too Small*
The Lost Purse	*When I Put My Hand in the Purse...*
In a Clown's Purse	*I Opened the Purse and Saw...*

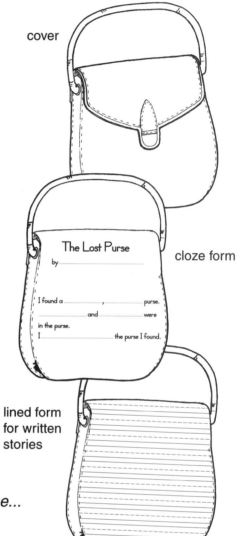

cover

cloze form

lined form for written stories

Group Books

- **Nurses' Purses—A Rhyming Book**
  Each student will need a blank purse form. Make several copies of the clip art on page 125. Brainstorm and create pairs of nouns that rhyme (nurse/purse, book/hook, etc.) Each student illustrates a rhyming pair of their choice on the blank form (or pastes a pair of rhyming objects from the clip art page). On the bottom of the page, they are to write a phrase or sentence about the picture. (*A book is hanging on a hook. A fish is on the dish.*) Compile student pages and attach a cover.

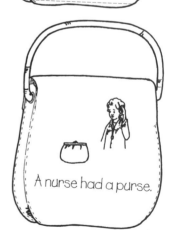

- **Purses**
  Extend the second activity on page 119 by having students write about a character's purse and what is in it. Students will need a blank purse form and a lined form. Students select a person, real or make-believe, and then draw and write about what that person might carry. Compile student pages and attach a cover.

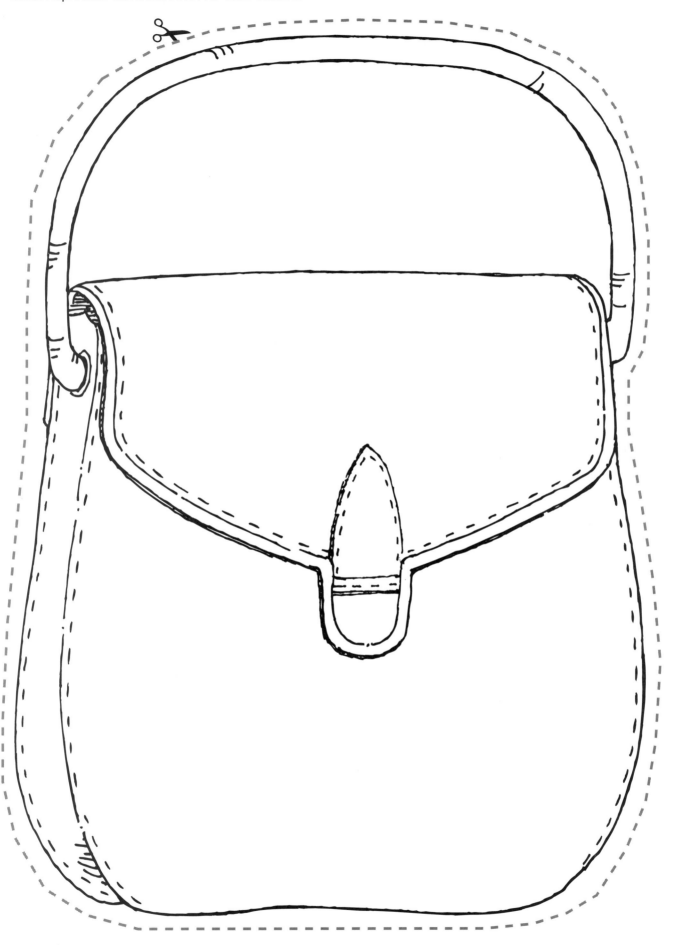

Note: Reproduce this page to draw a picture story or to use as a back cover.

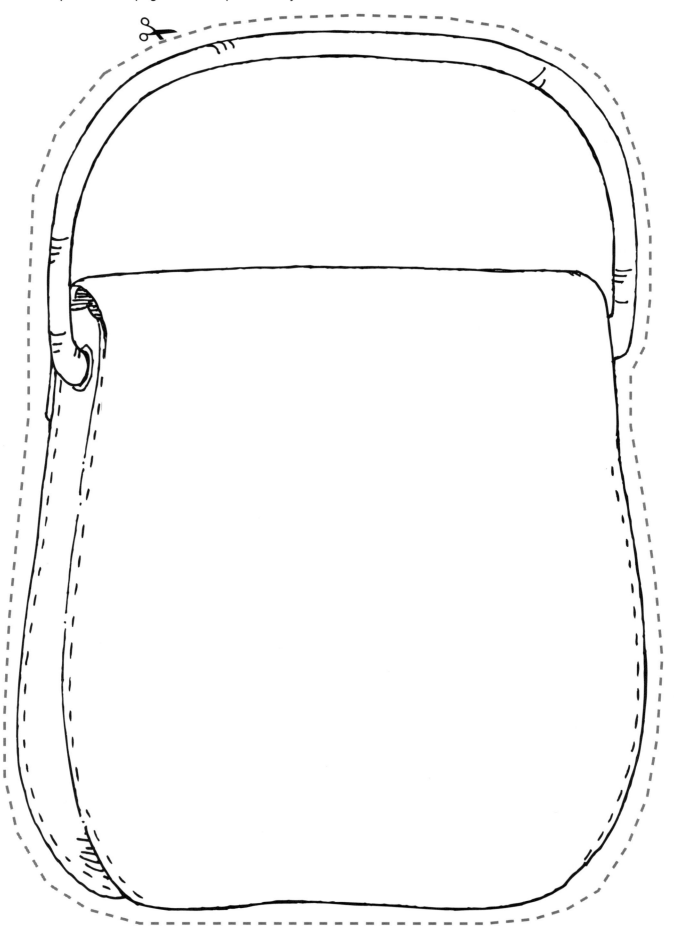

 Beginning Writers • EMC 776

The Lost Purse

by_____

I found a _____ , _____ purse.

_____ and _____ were

in the purse.

I _____ the purse I found.

Beginning Writers • EMC 776

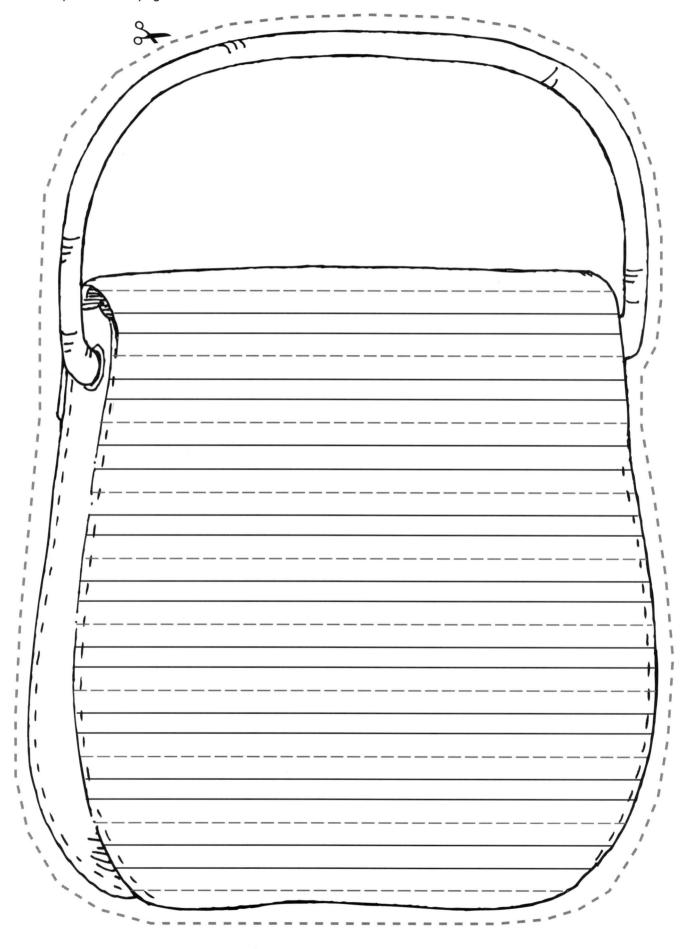

Note: Directions for using this clip art are on page 120.

Beginning Writers • EMC 776

Prewriting Activities

Read

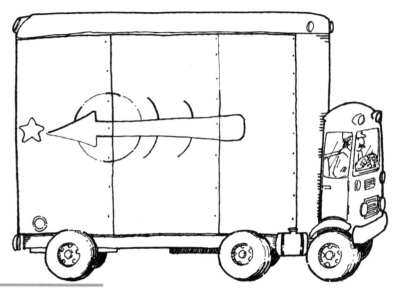

The Little Black Truck by Libba Moore Gray; Simon & Schuster, 1994.

Truck Trouble by Angela Toyston; DK Merchandise, 1998.

Trucks by Byron Barton; HarperCollins Juvenile Books, 1998.

Trucks by Gail Gibbons; HarperCollins Publishers, 1985.

My Trucks by Kirsten Hall; Children's Press, 1995.

Big Rigs by John Malam; Simon & Schuster, 1998.

Truck Song by Diane Siebert; Harper Trophy, 1987.

Get Ready to Write

1. Share a book about trucks with students. Discuss the different types of trucks. Ask students to name them and explain how they are used.

2. Bring in a variety of toy trucks and ask students to bring in toy trucks they have. Review the names of the various trucks and their functions. Put the toy trucks into categories by size, color, or function.

Writing Activities

Individual Books

- **Draw a Story**
  Reproduce the cover and several blank pages.
  Help students think of their own topics for stories
  or use one of the following ideas:

  Trucks
  Students are to draw one kind of truck on each page.

  Colorful Trucks
  Students are to draw a different colored truck on each
  page. Have them write the color of the truck at the
  bottom of each page.

- **Complete the Sentences**
  Reproduce the cover, a blank form, and the cloze form.
  Students complete the sentences to create a story and
  then draw a picture on the blank form.

- **Write a Story**
  Reproduce the cover and several lined forms. Students
  write their own truck stories. Possible story starters:

cover

cloze form

A Truck

by

I saw a _____ truck.
It was _____ and _____
I saw it _____

lined form for
written stories

All Aboard the Fire Truck	*Fun with Toy Trucks*
Gus, the Garbage Truck	*Farmer Fred's Pick-Up Truck*
If I Had a Truck, It Would Be...	*Red Truck, Blue Truck, Old Truck, New Truck*

Group Books

- **Where's the Truck—Positional Words**
  Each student will need a blank truck form and a truck
  from page 132. Brainstorm and list places the truck might
  be located (over the bridge, around the corner, up the hill,
  under a tree, on the truck scales, etc.). Students will color,
  cut out, and paste the truck to the blank form. They then
  draw the background to show where the truck is located
  and write a sentence describing the location of the truck.
  (*The garbage truck is in front of the house. My yellow fire
  truck is racing over the bridge.*) Compile student pages
  and attach a cover.

- **Trucks at Work**
  Each student will need one or more lined forms. Ask
  students to write fiction or nonfiction stories about a
  truck and the work it does. Compile student pages
  and attach a cover.

The fire truck went
down the street.

clip art

Note: Reproduce this book cover for each student.

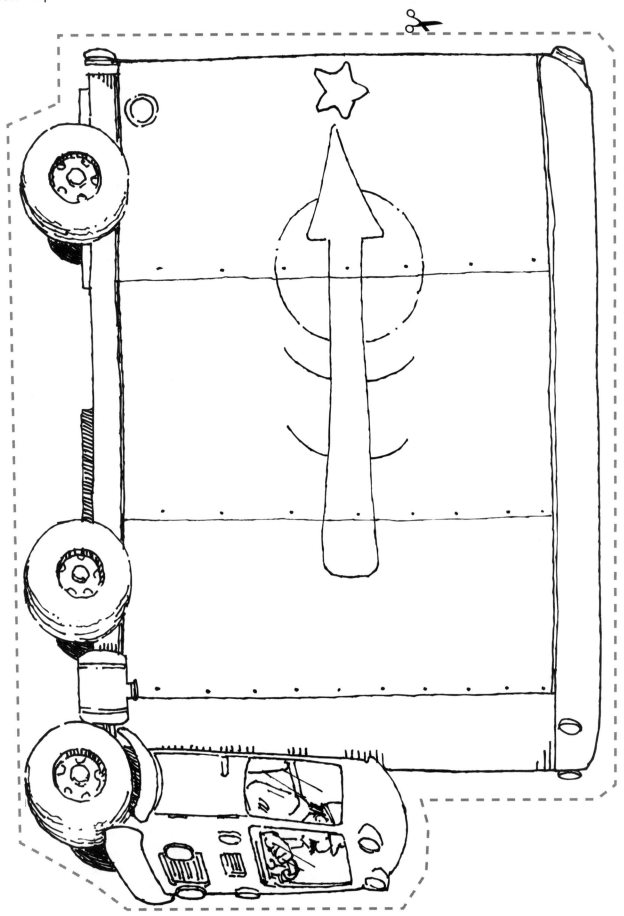

Note: Reproduce this page to draw a picture story or to use as a back cover.

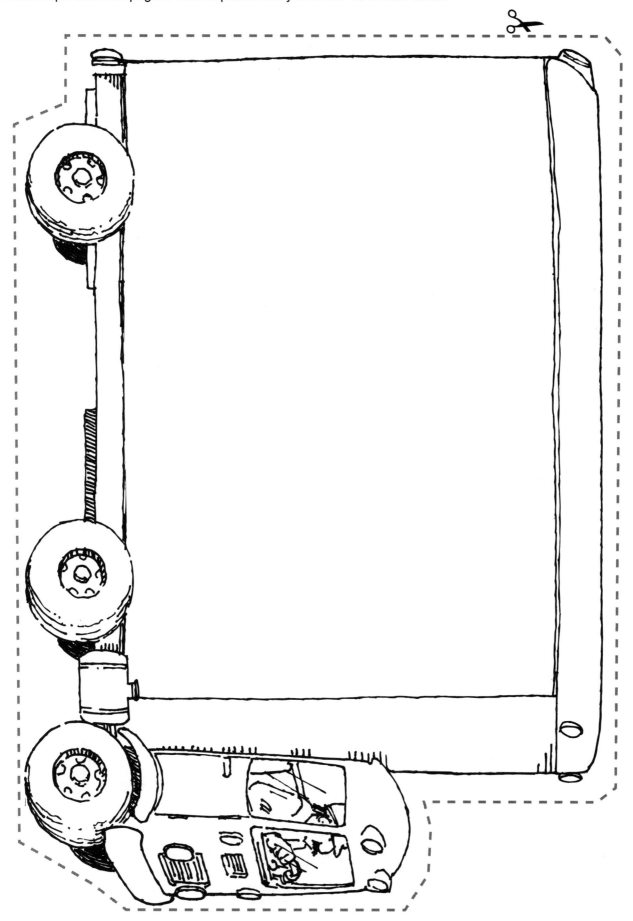

 Beginning Writers • EMC 776

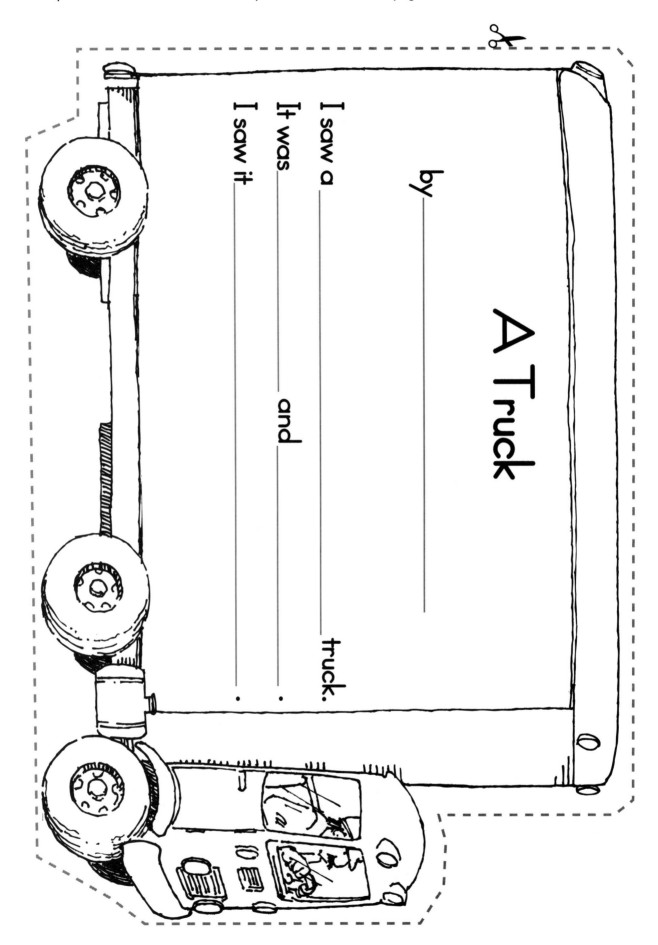

A Truck

by _____

I saw a _____ truck.

It was _____ and _____.

I saw it _____.

130

Note: Reproduce this page for written stories.

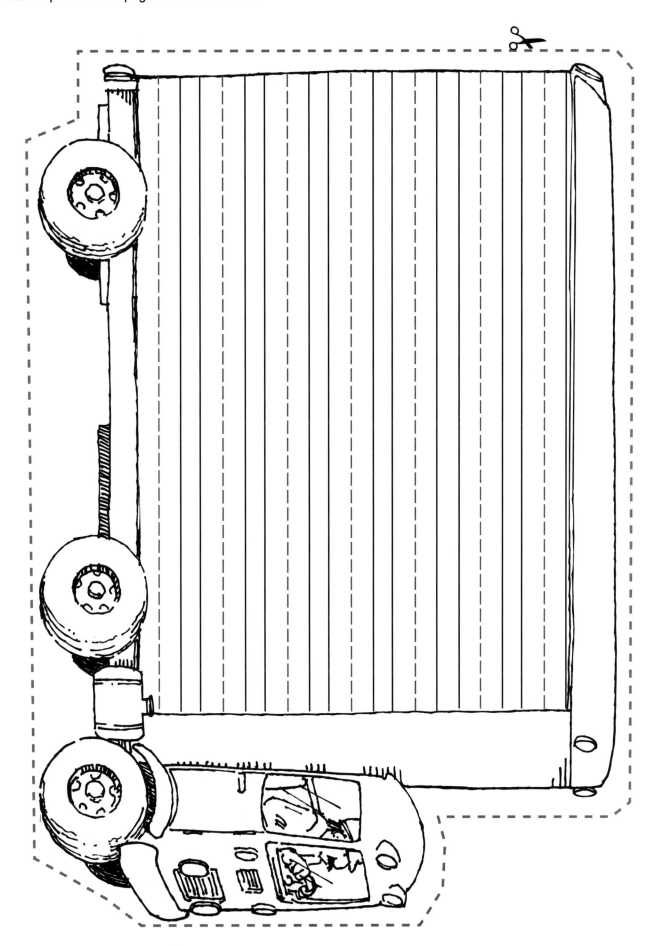

Note: Directions for using this clip art are on page 127.

132

Moon

Prewriting Activities

Read

I'll See You When the Moon Is Full by Susi Gregg
  Fowler; Greenwillow, 1994.

The Moon Book by Gail Gibbons; Holiday
  House, 1997.

Papa, Please Get the Moon for Me by
  Eric Carle; Simon & Schuster, 1991.

What Is the Full Moon Full Of? by
  Shulamith Levey Oppenheim; Boyds
  Mills Press, 1997.

Goodnight Moon by Margaret Wise Brown;
  HarperCollins Juvenile Books, 1991.

Grandpa Takes Me to the Moon by Timothy
  R. Gaffney; William Morrow, 1996.

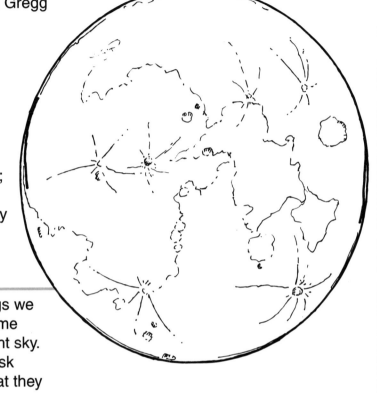

Get Ready to Write

1. Brainstorm and name some of the things we
   see in the night sky. Ask students to name
   the largest or brightest object in the night sky.
   After someone has named the moon, ask
   students to describe it and to share what they
   know about the moon.

2. Share a book that presents the phases of the
   moon, such as *The Moon Book* by Gail Gibbons.
   Discuss what the moon looks like at different
   times of the month as it changes shape.

Writing Activites

Individual Books

• **Draw a Story**

Reproduce the cover and several blank pages.
Help students think of their own topics for stories
or use one of the following ideas:

I See the Moon
Students draw a different view of the moon
on each page.

M Is for Moon
On each page students draw a different object beginning
with the sound of letter /m/.

• **Complete the Sentences**

Reproduce the cover, a blank form, and the cloze form.
Students draw a picture on the blank form and complete
the sentences to create a story telling the time the moon
is seen, what it looks like, and something it does.

• **Write a Story**

Reproduce the cover and several lined forms. Students
write their own moon stories. Possible story starters:

The Moon	*If the Moon Could Talk*
The Moon Changes	*The Man in the Moon*
Playing in the Moonlight	*The Moon Is Made of* ____

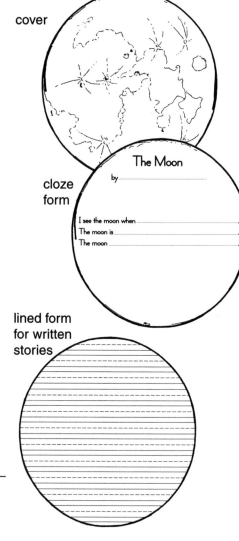

cover

cloze form

The Moon

by

I see the moon when
The moon is
The moon

lined form for written stories

Group Books

• **A Trip to the Moon**

Reproduce a blank moon form, a lined form, and the clip
art on page 139 for each student. They are to color and cut
out the astronaut and lunar rover and paste them to the blank
form. Add details with crayons. Then they will write a story
about a trip to the moon. Place the finished stories in
a cover.

• **Strange Footsteps on the Moon**

Students will need one or more lined moon forms and a
"strange footprint" from page 139. They are to paste the
footprint to their writing form and then write a funny
or scary story about the creature that made the
strange footprint.

A Trip to the Moon

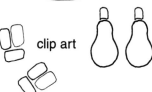

clip art

Note: Reproduce this book cover for each student.

 Beginning Writers • EMC 776

Note: Reproduce this page to draw a picture story or to use as a back cover.

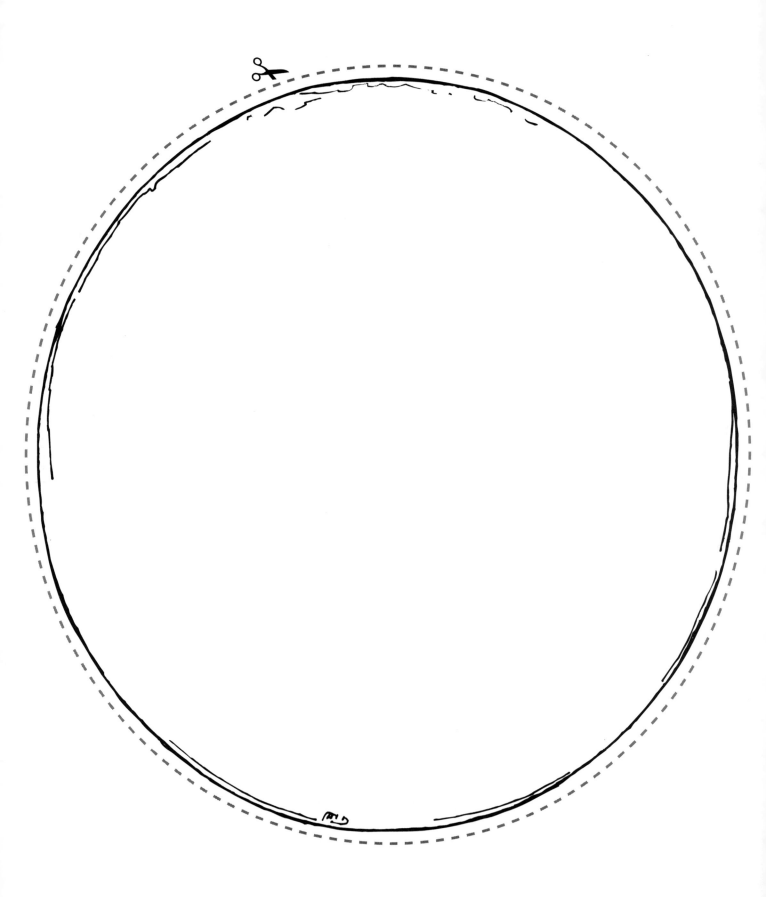

Beginning Writers • EMC 776

The Moon

by _____

I see the moon when _____ .

The moon is _____ .

The moon _____ .

Beginning Writers • EMC 776

Note: Reproduce this page for written stories.

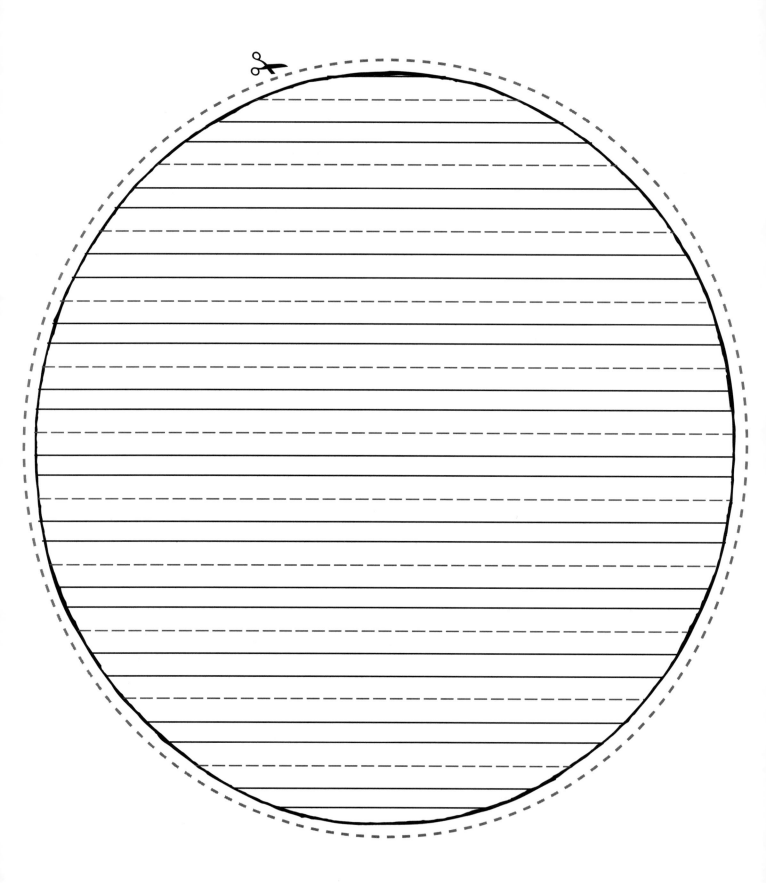

Note: Directions for using this clip art are on page 134.

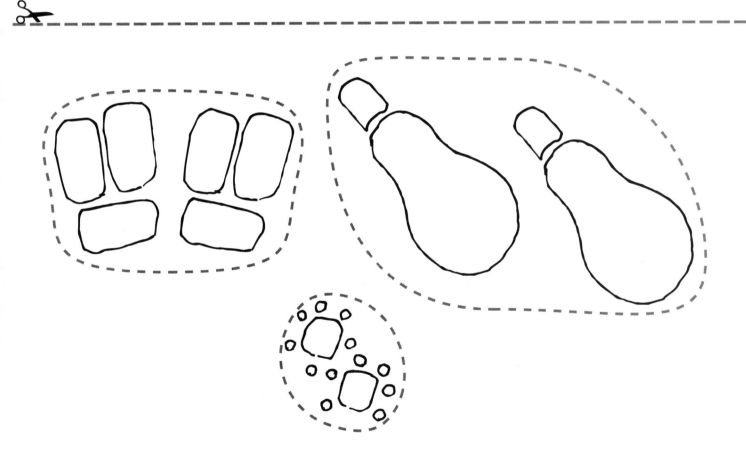

Bucket

Prewriting Activities

Read

There's a Hole in My Bucket by Ingrid Schubert and Dieter Schubert; Front Street Press, 1998.

Sophie's Bucket by Catherine Stock; Harcourt Brace, 1994.

At the Beach by Anne F. Rockwell; Aladdin Paperbacks, 1991.

The Puddle Pail by Elisa Kleven; Dutton Books, 1997.

Get Ready to Write

1. Bring in an assortment of buckets and pails (metal bucket, mop bucket, plastic pail, toy bucket and shovel). Ask students to describe the buckets and to think of ways each one might be used.

2. Poke a hole near the bottom of an inexpensive plastic bucket. Challenge students to think of things you could carry in the bucket despite the hole. Then ask them to think of ways you could fix the bucket so you could carry sand or water without it leaking out.

Writing Activities

Individual Books

• **Draw a Story**
Reproduce the cover and several blank pages.
Help students think of their own topics for stories
or use one of the following ideas:

In My Bucket
Students are to draw a different object in each pail.

A (color word) Bucket
Give each student one or more blank pages. They
are to select one color for each page and draw
objects of only that color in the bucket. Have them
write the color word on the page.

• **Complete the Sentences**
Reproduce the cover, a blank form, and the cloze form.
Students complete the sentences to create a story and
then draw a picture on the blank form.

• **Write a Story**
Reproduce the cover and several lined forms. Students
write their own bucket stories. Possible story starters:

My Bucket Has a Hole in It	*Pet in a Pail*
I Used My Bucket...	*A Purple Plastic Pail*
What Crawled Out of the Bucket?	*Seashore Collection*

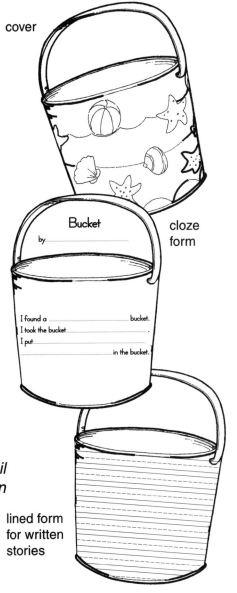

cover

cloze
form

lined form
for written
stories

Group Books

• **Bucket, Bucket, How Many In the Bucket?**
Each student will need a blank bucket form and a copy
of the clip art on page 146. Assign each student a number.
Each is to show this number using a combination of all
three objects (for example, 3 tadpoles, 2 frogs, 1 fish for
6; or 4 fish, 1 frog, 1 tadpole for 6). Students then write
an addition sentence about the objects (for example,
3 + 2 + 1 = 6). Compile student pages and attach a cover.

• **At the Beach**
Students will need one or more lined forms. Brainstorm
and list ways a bucket at the beach (carry water, build a
sand castle, collect shells, etc.) might be used. Have
students write a story to tell about using their bucket.
Compile student stories and attach a cover.

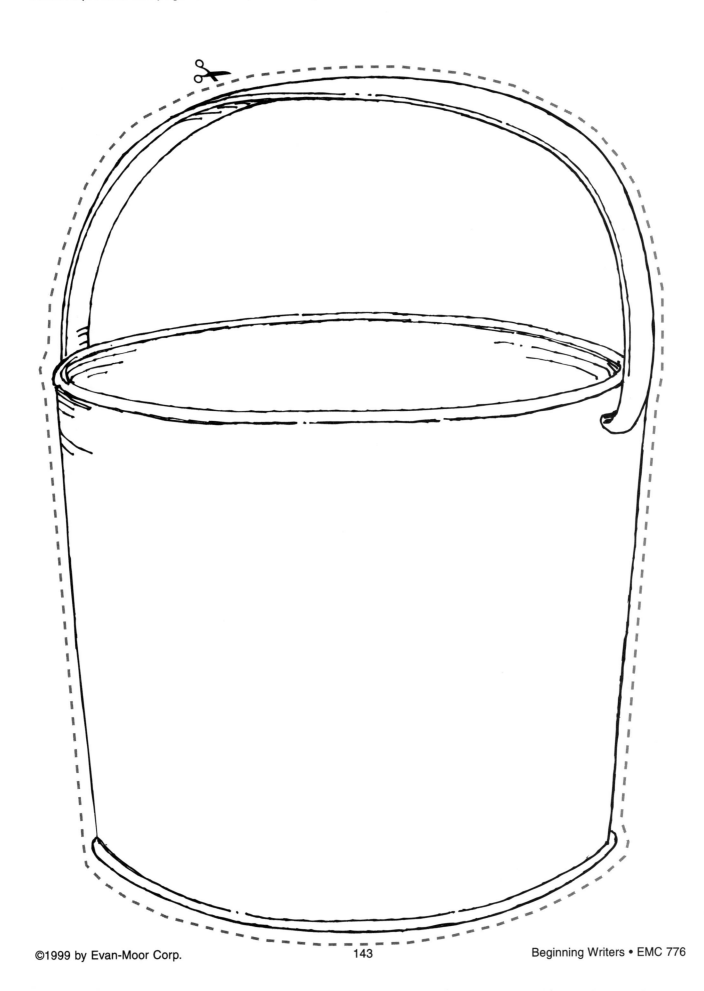

Bucket

by_____

I found a _____ bucket.

I took the bucket_____ .

I put_____

_____ in the bucket.

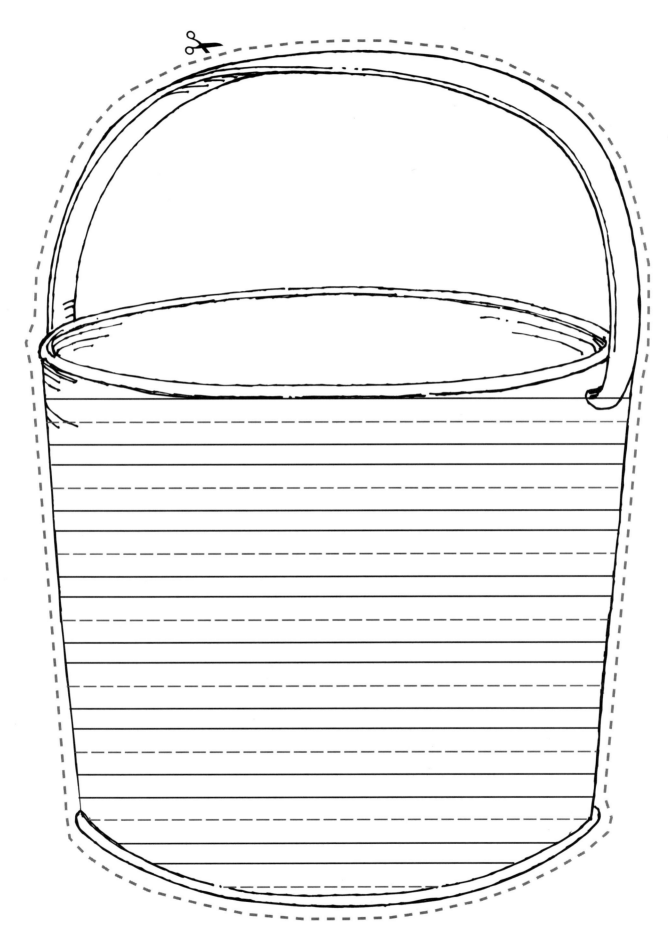

Note: Directions for using this clip art are on page 141.

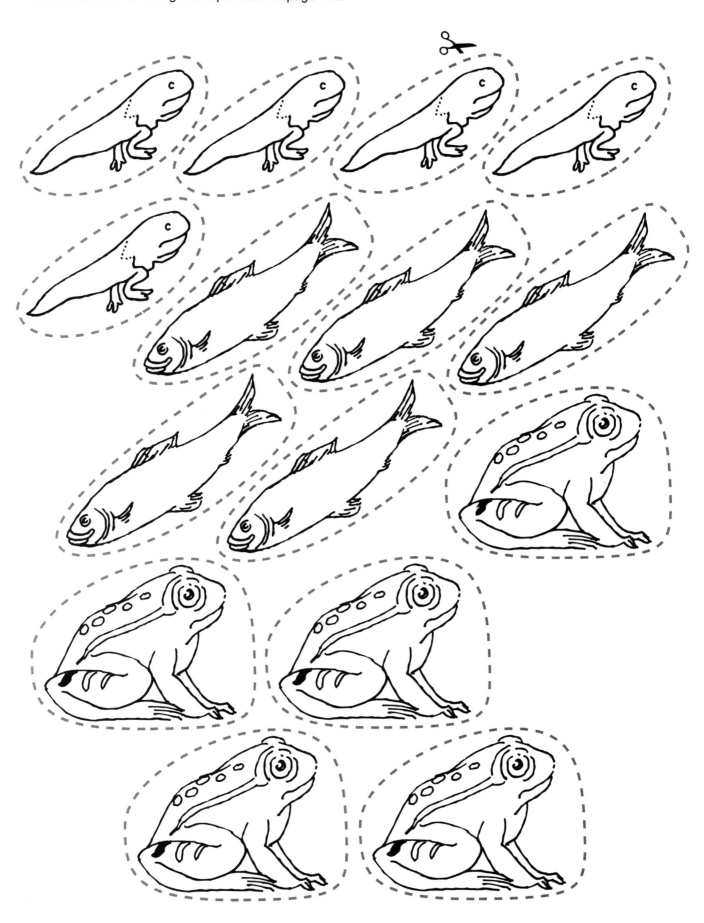

 Beginning Writers • EMC 776

Prewriting Activities

Read

A Nest Full of Eggs by Priscilla Belz Jenkins;
Harper Trophy, 1995.
The Magpies' Nest by Joanna Foster;
Clarion Books, 1995.
Dora's Eggs by Julie Sykes; Little Tiger
Press, 1998.
Best Nest by Philip D. Eastman;
Random Library, 1991.
Birds' Nest by Barrie Watts; Silver
Burdett Press, 1990.

Get Ready to Write

1. Read and discuss a book about different
   kinds of nests. What are the nests
   made of? Who builds the nests? What
   is a nest used for? Share a real nest if
   possible. Have students look closely to
   identify the types of items the bird used
   to construct the nest.

2. Check your audiovisual catalog
   to find a filmstrip or video showing a bird
   building a nest. Show this to your students
   before they begin writing about nests.

Writing Activities

Individual Books

• Draw a Story

Reproduce the cover and several blank pages.
Help students think of their own topics for stories
or use one of the following ideas:

cover

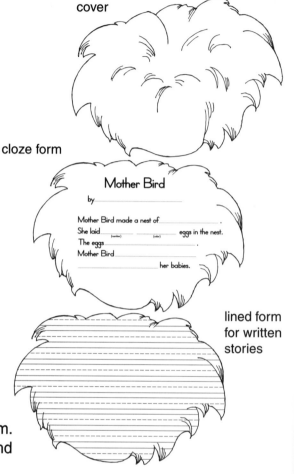

cloze form

1, 2, 3 Eggs in a Nest
Students will need three blank forms and
a bird from page 153. They are to draw one egg
in the first nest, two eggs in the second nest, and
three eggs in the third nest. Label each page with
a number and the word "eggs." Color, cut out, and
paste the mother bird to the last nest.

Mother Bird, Baby Bird
Discuss ways a mother bird cares for her babies
(builds a safe nest, brings them food, protects
them from other birds or cats). On blank forms,
have students illustrate one or more ways a mother
bird cares for her babies.

lined form
for written
stories

• Complete the Sentences

Reproduce the cover, a blank form, and the cloze form.
Students complete the sentences to create a story and
then draw a picture on the blank form.

• Write a Story

Reproduce the cover and several lined forms. Students
write their own nest and bird stories. Possible story starters:

A Nest in a Hat	*I Peeked into a Nest and Saw...*
The Best Nest	*When Will It Hatch?*
How to Build a Nest	*I Woke Up in a Nest*

Group Books

• Birds on a Nest

Share books about various birds, their nests, and their eggs. Give
each student a blank form, a lined form, and a bird from page 153.
They are to draw eggs in the nest and then color, cut out, and glue the bird to the nest. Write
about the bird and its nest on their lined form. Compile student pages and attach a cover.

• Something Strange in the Bird's Nest

Students will need one or more lined forms. Discuss what unusual items might be found in a
bird's nest (an unusual egg, a strange animal, some object the bird picked up, etc.). Students
are to write about one unusual thing, how it got in the nest, and what happened to it. Compile
student pages and attach a cover.

Note: Reproduce this page to draw a picture story or to use as a back cover.

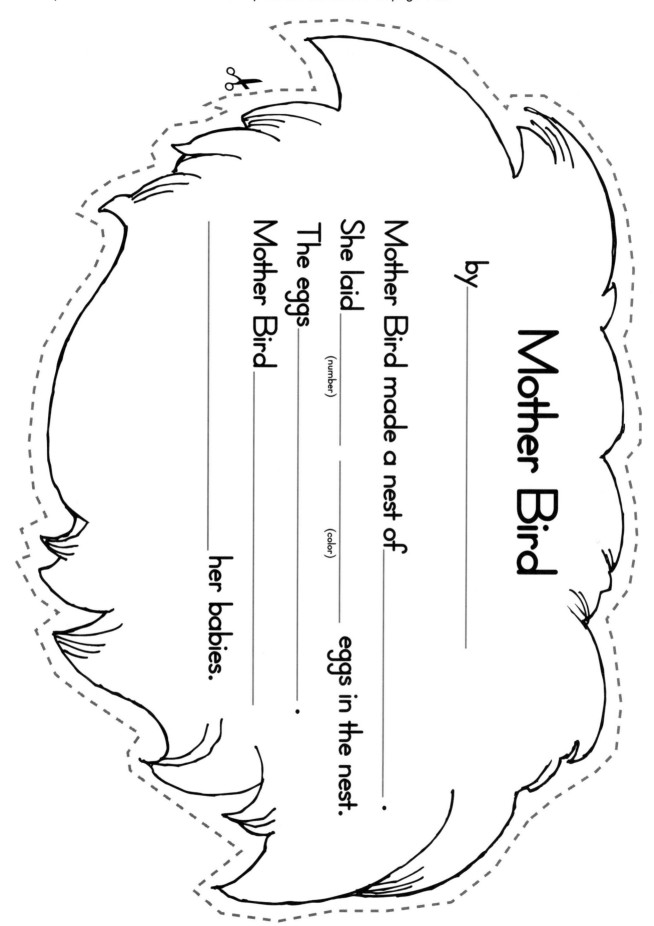

Mother Bird

by _____

Mother Bird made a nest of _____.

She laid _____ eggs in the nest.
(number)

The eggs _____.
(color)

Mother Bird _____ her babies.

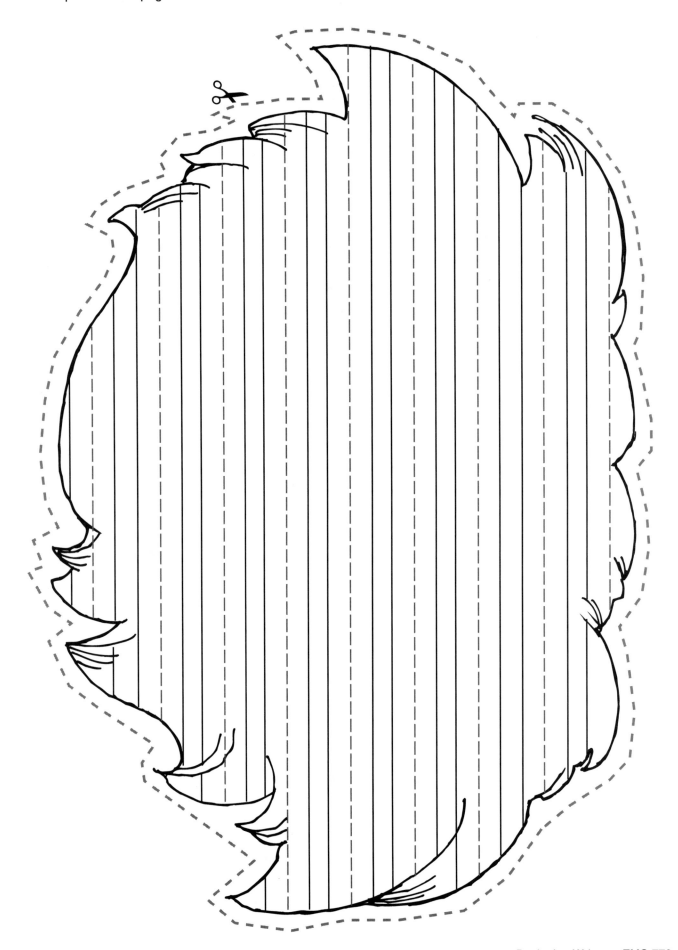

Note: Directions for using this clip art are on page 148.

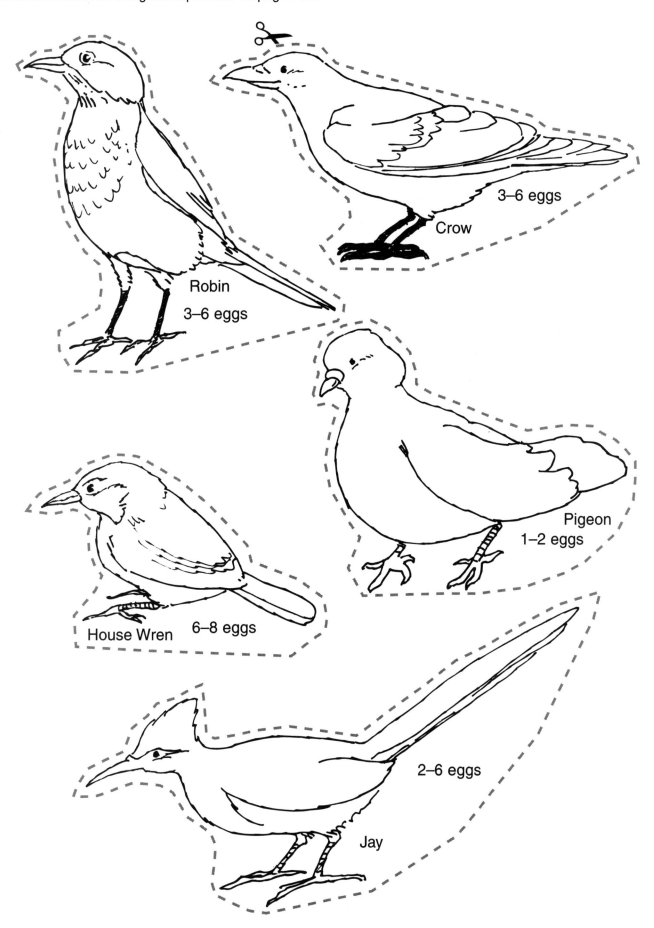

Robin
3–6 eggs

Crow
3–6 eggs

House Wren
6–8 eggs

Pigeon
1–2 eggs

Jay
2–6 eggs

 Beginning Writers • EMC 776

Camping

Prewriting Activities

Read

Sleep Out by Carol Carrick; Houghton Mifflin Company, 1982.

Acorn Magic by Maggie Stern; Greenwillow, 1998.

Chicago and the Cat: The Camping Trip by Robin Michal Koontz; Puffin, 1997.

When Daddy Took Us Camping by Julie Brillhart; Albert Whitman & Company, 1997.

Amelia Bedelia Goes Camping by Peggy Parish; Camelot, 1997.

Bailey Goes Camping by Kevin Henkes; Mulberry Books, 1997.

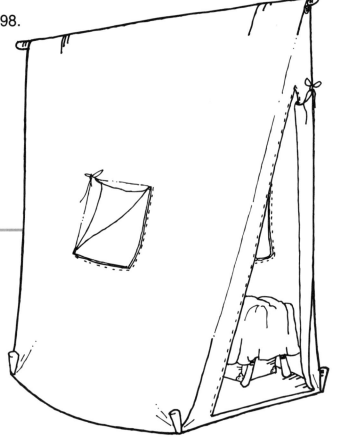

Get Ready to Write

1. Pitch a tent in the classroom. This can be as simple as a blanket spread over a table, or you can set up a real tent. Have students gather around the tent as they share their camping experiences. Brainstorm the types of things you take camping (tent, lantern, camp stove, sleeping bag, etc.). Discuss the types of things you might do when camping (hike, fish, cook over a campfire, etc.).

2. Make a "Yes-No" graph showing how many students have or have not been camping.

Writing Activities

Individual Books

cover

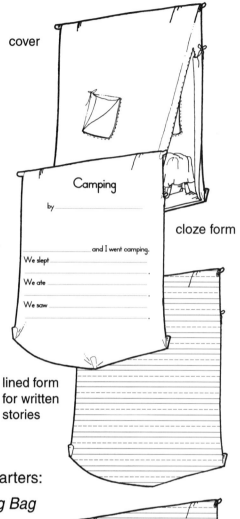

Camping

by _____

_____ and I went camping.

We slept _____

We ate _____

We saw _____

cloze form

lined form for written stories

• **Draw a Story**
Reproduce the cover and several blank pages.
Help students think of their own topics for stories
or use one of the following ideas:

Camping
Students draw one or more pictures of themselves
camping (sleeping in a sleeping bag, sitting by the
tent, hiking among the trees). Staple the pictures
with a cover.

Who Went Camping?
On each blank page, students draw a different
picture of who went camping (Dad, Aunt Ethel,
the family dog, Baby Sister, etc.). Write the
person's name under each picture.

• **Complete the Sentences**
Reproduce the cover, a blank form, and the cloze form.
Students complete the sentences to create a story and
then draw a picture on the blank form.

• **Write a Story**
Reproduce the cover and several lined forms. Students
write their own tent and camping stories. Possible story starters:

Camping with Grandma   *A Surprise in My Sleeping Bag*
Sleeping in the Backyard   *If I Could Go Camping...*
What Lifted the Tent Flap?   *Pitching a Tent*

This is a flashlight.
It has a bulb. I use it
when I need to see
at night.

Group Books

• **A Camping Dictionary**
Reproduce a lined tent form for each student and several copies
of the clip art on page 160. Each student selects one item of
camping equipment. They draw (or cut and paste) the item to
the top of the writing form. Students then write a description
of the item, including its name, what it is made of, and how
it is used. Compile student pages and attach a cover.

• **Noises in the Night—A Camping Adventure**
Reproduce one or more lined tent forms for each student.
Brainstorm and list noises they might hear at night while
camping. Each student then writes a camping story in which
a night noise leads to an adventure. Compile student stories
and attach a cover.

clip art

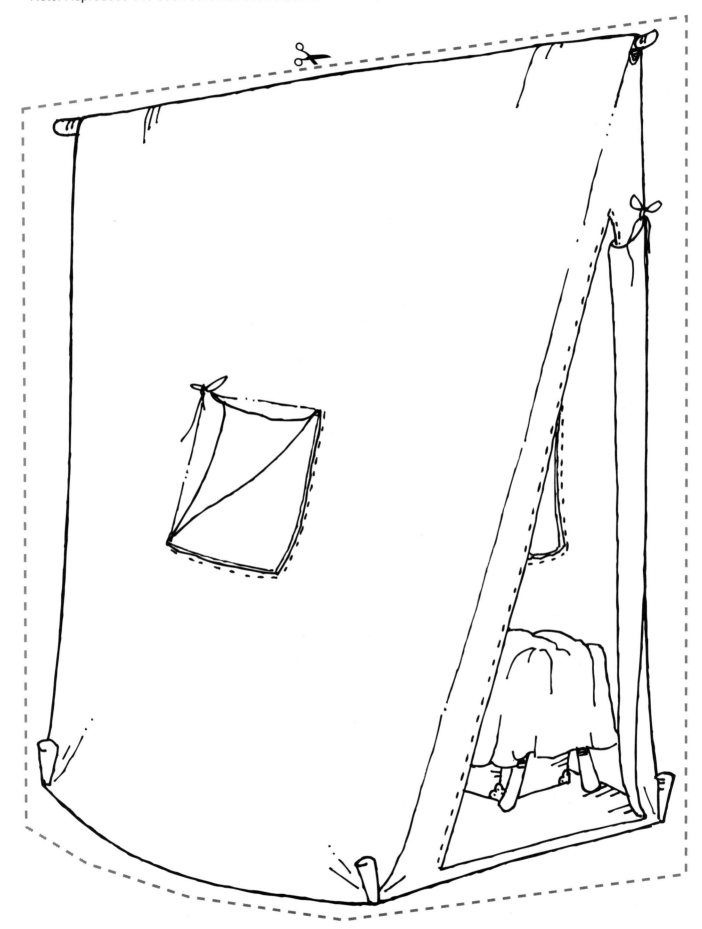

Note: Reproduce this page to draw a picture story or to use as a back cover.

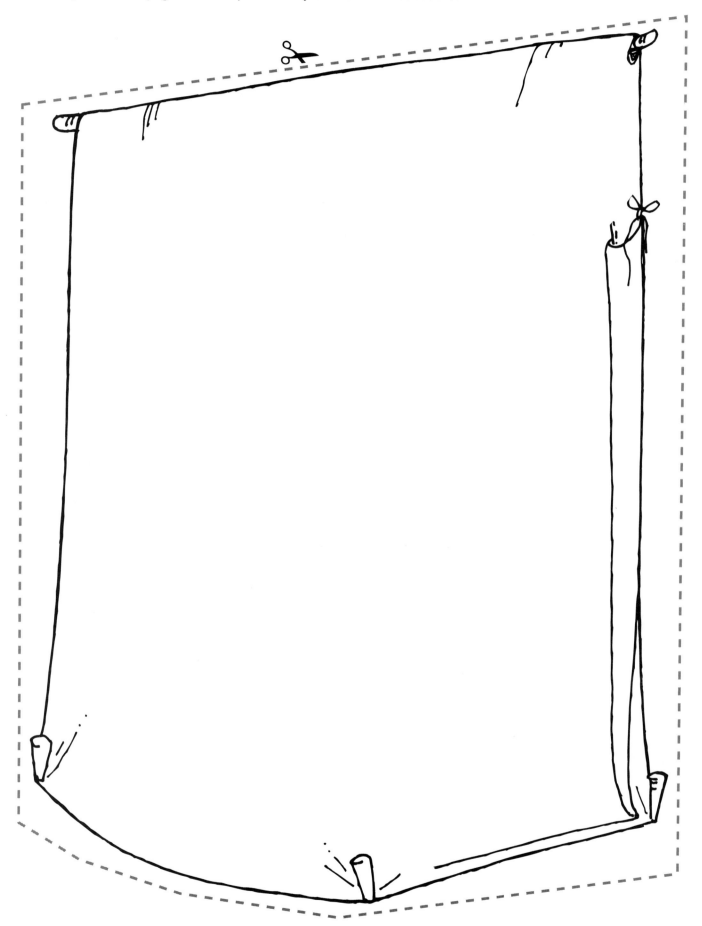

Camping

by _____

_____ and I went camping.

We slept _____

_____ .

We ate _____

_____ .

We saw _____

_____ .

Note: Directions for using this clip art are on page 155.

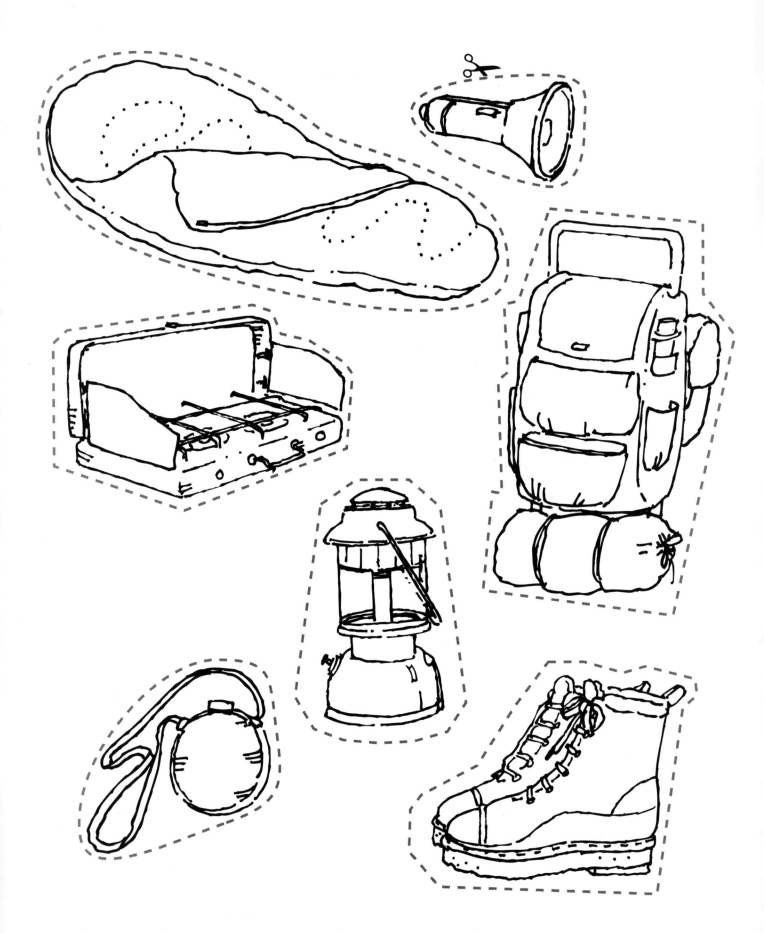

Beginning Writers • EMC 776